George Mounfell Boon
10. v. 1949.

# TOPOGRAPHY
## OF
# ROMAN SCOTLAND

# TOPOGRAPHY

## OF

# ROMAN SCOTLAND

*North of the Antonine Wall*

BY

O. G. S. CRAWFORD

CAMBRIDGE
At the University Press
1949

*Printed in Great Britain at the University Press, Cambridge*
*(Brooke Crutchley, University Printer)*
*and published by the Cambridge University Press*
*(Cambridge, and Bentley House, London)*

*Agents for U.S.A., Canada, and India:  Macmillan*

# Contents

# Illustrations

## PLATES

*(Plates I—XXI will be found at the end of the book)*

## FIGURES IN THE TEXT

# Abbreviations

| | |
|---|---|
| *P.S.A.S.* | *Proceedings of the Society of Antiquaries of Scotland.* |
| *J.R.S.* | *Journal of the Roman Society.* |
| *O.E.D.* | *Oxford English Dictionary.* |
| *O.S.A.* | *Old Statistical Account.* |
| *N.S.A.* | *New Statistical Account.* |
| O.S. | Ordnance Survey. |
| *Itin. Sept.* | *Itinerarium Septentrionale* (Gordon, 1726). |
| Forfarshire | The name has been changed to Angus, but the older name still appears on most of the 6 in. maps, and is therefore used in this book. |

# Preface

The contents of this book were delivered as the Rhind Lectures in Edinburgh, in October and November 1943. The style has been left unaltered, except for some necessary verbal changes, in the hope that the book may thereby be found more readable. Except for purposes of illustration in the first chapter, I have dealt only with Scotland north of the Antonine Wall (i.e. the Forth-Clyde line). The results of my field-work south of it will be incorporated in part of a monograph dealing with the Roman occupation of south-western Scotland, which is being prepared for publication by the Glasgow Archaeological Society.

My debt to colleagues past and present will at once be clear. Like all students of Roman Britain, I owe much to the late Sir George Macdonald, and it is to him that I owe the possibility of writing this book. I am greatly indebted to my former colleague, Mr W. F. Grimes, now Keeper of the London Museum, for having most kindly drawn so many of the plans (Figs. 3, 5, 9, 12, 13, 20–25, 28, 31, 32 and the Index map at the end).

I wish also to acknowledge with many thanks the permission given me (1) by Mr Ian Richmond to reproduce his work in Figs. 6, 10, 11, 16, 17, 18, 19 and the splendid plan of Fendoch facing p. 46; (2) by the Council of the Society of Antiquaries of Scotland to reproduce Figs. 7, 11, 14, 16–18, 27, 30 and the plan of Fendoch; (3) by the Council of the Society of Roman Studies to reproduce Figs. 1, 2, 8, 10, 17, 19; (4) by the Librarian of Perth to reproduce on Plates VI, XIII and XX facsimiles of old maps there; (5) by the Council of the British Archaeological Institute to reproduce Fig. 6; (6) by Professor W. D. Simpson to reproduce Fig. 29; (7) by Mr Geoffrey Alington to reproduce Plate V. Other photographs of Roman sites in Scotland, taken during a flight in 1939, will be found in *Antiquity*, XIII (Sept. 1939), pp. 280–92: 'An Air Reconnaissance of Roman Scotland.'

To Mr Eric Bradley are due the air-photographs appearing on Plates XI, XVI, and I wish to thank him for the use of them.

My own contribution consists in the field-work and library work necessary to write a book like this. Field-work is rather like an ice-berg—the proportion of what eventually appears to what lies concealed is small—to establish one genuine Roman site one may have to visit many false claimants. Most of the photographs also are my own. The plans have been copied from the first edition of the 6 in. map, in which there is no copyright. The archaeological information there given is generally better than that on the later editions; there was very little revision between 1920 and 1939, except of urban districts.

Finally, I wish to thank the staff of the Cambridge University Press for all they have done to help in producing the book and for their patience and efficiency.

O. G. S. CRAWFORD

NURSLING
1 *March* 1948

# Chapter One

## ROMAN CAMPS, FORTS & ROADS

THERE is nothing quite so exciting as following a newly discovered Roman road across country. It is a form of sport with its own technique and, other things being equal, success comes most readily to the best technician. But the conscientious description of its course is apt to be less exciting—at any rate for the reader, for I have found it interesting enough to write. Perhaps the fact that (in spite of the numerous literary references) it is essentially an 'open air' book may make it readable, if only for those who know the country. Before setting out on the journey, however, it will be as well to give a short account of its plan. There is first a little ground to be cleared by way of general explanations, for the true nature of Roman field-remains is not sufficiently well known for me to assume it. We shall then start at the Roman fort of Camelon near Falkirk and follow the Roman road, which was also the line of the Roman advance, northwards by Stirling, through Strathallan, Strathearn and Strathmore to Stonehaven, and by Inverurie to the northernmost known Roman camp at Glenmailen, and thence to the shores of the Moray Firth. The Roman road is lost beyond Kirriemuir, and no permanent fort has been discovered further north than Cardean near Meigle.

There is one outstanding distinction between the earthworks of the Romans and those of their native enemies: the former are all military and invariably conform to a pattern laid down by regulations. If they had only realized this simple fact, the earlier antiquaries would have been saved from innumerable errors. The essential difference is between the carefully planned, regular, straight-sided camps and forts built by the civilized Roman soldiers, and the irregular hill-forts of the barbarians they were fighting. So too, a Roman road was a carefully aligned and constructed metalled causeway, whose course was laid out from one high point to another. The Roman roads and forts of Scotland are exactly comparable to those made there by the English in the eighteenth century. An even closer analogy is with the roads constructed by their modern descendants in Abyssinia, where the occupation was even shorter and certainly quite as uncomfortable.

Roman military sites consist of general headquarters, called legionary forts, of which there is only one (Inchtuthil) in our region, large permanent

forts, smaller forts and fortlets, and signal-posts. There are also temporary
marching-camps of two kinds, large and small, such as were made at
intervals of a day's march during the first advance. It is to be presumed
that, in order of construction, the marching-camps came first, followed
during the period of consolidation by the forts and roads. Certainly the
smaller forts and fortlets and signal-posts were in some cases made when the
exact course of the road had already been fixed. Roman forts are nearly
always rectangular, and their corners are rounded, this last being a valuable
diagnostic feature differentiating Roman earthworks from those of other
periods. Rectangular earthworks at Fortingall, Ardargie (Perthshire),
Fordoun (Kincardineshire) and Templand (Dumfriesshire) have all been
claimed as Roman, but are probably of medieval origin. All four have
sharp, not rounded, corners, and those at Fortingall and Fordoun both have
wet moats fed by an artificial stream—a feature characteristic of medieval
homestead moats in the south of England.

The entrances of marching-camps are protected by a bank and ditch in
front of them called a *tutulus* or traverse. This is a valuable means of identification. Sometimes it survives when the line of the rampart and ditch itself
has been destroyed, as at Oathlaw near Forfar.

Another feature which distinguishes Roman from native earthwork is its
rigid mathematical straightness. Even on the ground it is generally easy to
recognize; it is the hall-mark of the disciplined civilized army—if one can
call an army civilized—as against the easygoing wobbly line of the un-
disciplined barbarian. Such for instance is the direct unwavering alignment
of the Cleaven Dyke which may be contrasted with the irregular linear
earthwork near Melrose.[1] From the air this characteristic feature is instantly
recognizable, and in those instances where I have used it to determine the
character of the remains, I have never yet had a failure when my opinion has
been tested by excavation. On an air-photograph it is, in fact, as easy to
distinguish characteristic Roman from native earthwork as to tell a Bronze-
Age beaker from a Samian bowl.

Few of the Roman sites in our region are at all well preserved. Camelon
has a factory covering one-half of it and a ploughed field the other. The
ramparts of Ardoch are fairly perfect, but the interior of the fort has
been ploughed. Strageath has long been under cultivation but is still
recognizable in parts. Dalginross was once cultivated and is probably now
ploughed up again. Fendoch, 'Bertha' and Cardean have all been ploughed.

1 See *Antiquity*, x (1936), pp. 346–9.

Inchtuthil has been disfigured (since I first visited it) by a private golf-course. The problematic site near Fochabers has reverted to its presumed original purpose. The marching-camps of Lintrose, Kirkbuddo, Glenmailen and Raedykes still show fragments of ramparts, the last two quite considerable fragments; but of the two marching-camps near Forfar and Brechin nothing survives but a single traverse. The bulk of this destruction has been done within the last two centuries. In General Roy's time there was much more left; and had it not been for his indefatigable work and the plans he made we should probably never have known of the existence of many of the sites.

No one could possibly wish to see a perfect earthwork subjected to cultivation; but since the application of air-photography to ancient sites it is arguable that a *short* period under certain crops might be of advantage to some sites if properly exploited. Such sites are those which have already been under plough and reverted to grass again. In these cases the pristine sharpness of outline is gone for ever, and the grass veils all details even from the air-camera, except under certain special conditions of vegetation, soil and drought. All traces of the ramparts have already been obliterated; but we might learn a great deal about the internal plan if the site were ploughed up for a few successive years and sown with selected crops. Air-photographs taken at regular intervals would be instructive, and we should learn even from our failures. I first made this suggestion many years ago, and I make it again without having the slightest expectation that it will be carried out. It has recently been made again by Mr Richmond.

Finally, a few words about Roman roads. Few subjects would appear to be so easy to understand, yet few are less understood. The popular idea is that all Roman roads are paved, presumably with flat slabs like those of which street pavements are made. Instances of such paving do occur in other countries where suitable stone is available near at hand: the Appian Way from Rome to the Alban Hills is paved with blocks of lava. There are even a few instances in Britain—the road over the Whitby moors and over Blackstone Edge. And there is a paved Roman ford in the Weald of Sussex, to prevent the carts loaded with iron ore getting stuck in the mud; the road itself is made of iron ore. There seem to be quite a number of paved roads in the Forest of Dean, another iron-mining region in Roman times; but, although I believe some, or all, of them may well prove to be Roman, that must be left to some future investigator to prove, for it is still a virgin forest as far as archaeology is concerned. But there are no paved Roman roads known in Scotland where, as elsewhere, the normal Roman road was just a metalled road. It is not the metalling which is usually most conspicuous now, however, but rather the raised causeway on which it was laid. It is that causeway which we follow across country when we are tracing the course of a Roman road. We look for evidence of it; and without such evidence we are not entitled to regard the existence of a Roman road as proven. There are, of course, other subsidiary kinds of evidence, such as parish boundaries, straight hedge-lines and the like, which may be used by the discerning; and there may be explicit references to 'streets' in medieval documents. I do not, however, propose to deal with this kind of evidence here, partly because it applies more to the south of England than to our less-documented northern lands, partly because I have already dealt with it at some length in a book, *Man and his Past*, written during the 1914–18 war and now reprinted.

Let me repeat that the evidence for a Roman road is the existence of a causeway, a broad low mound of earth, about 16 ft. wide in its perfect state. Plate I shows a section of the Roman road near Glenochar in Lanarkshire. The causeway consists of rubble mixed with some large stones, resting on gritty boulder-clay. The exposure is in the side of a pit, and prolonged weathering has brought out well the distinction between the artificial soil and the natural deposit below on which it rests. The materials of the causeway were obtained by digging pits by the side of the road, so that it may consist of any sort of materials. These quarries are in fact most valuable clues to look for in tracing the course of the road. They can be seen in clusters on both sides of the road which runs over the moors near Moffat.[1] One of the best examples of these quarry-pits is to be found 10 miles south of Edinburgh, on the Biggar road between Silverburn and Carlops, on a rocky ridge between the Quarrel Burn on the north-west and the main road near Braidwood. Here the causeway itself is almost completely lost, and I was in some doubt whether I was following the correct line, when I noticed two parallel rows of pits running on either side. When seen subsequently from the air they were most strikingly plain and clear, and the causeway between them was also just visible.

Unfortunately, not all disused causeway-roads can be accepted as Roman. Such roads were made in Scotland, mostly during the eighteenth century, and it is sometimes extremely difficult to distinguish them from Roman roads. Here again the quarries help. The eighteenth-century road-makers

1 See *Antiquity*, XIII (1939), p. 280, Plate III.

obtained their materials, not from a large number of small pits dug all along the sides of the road, as did the Romans, but from a smaller number of larger pits dug into the slope of the hillside. Plate II shows such a pit on Mendick Hill near Dolphinton, where the issue is complicated by the fact that a genuine Roman road runs almost parallel to a causeway-road of the eighteenth century, the predecessor of the existing Biggar road. The same duplication is found near Beattock Summit, between Moffat and Crawford, where the eighteenth-century hillside quarries occur at intervals of almost a quarter of a mile apart.

As I have already said, it is extremely difficult, and sometimes impossible, to decide whether any given isolated portion of a causeway is of Roman or eighteenth-century construction. There are certain features, however, which if discernible may help. The eighteenth-century causeways generally have rather sharply defined edges, consisting of small scarped slopes, 2 ft. wide, on either side. This is particularly noticeable when the road runs along the side of a gently sloping hill, as near the Beef-tub (Plate III). The edges of a Roman causeway, on the contrary, merge almost imperceptibly into the ground on either side, and for that reason are almost impossible to illustrate by photography. And here I would take the opportunity of saying that the whole subject-matter of this book—roads and earthworks—consists of objects which are extremely difficult to photograph, at any rate on the ground; and also that, for illustrating these preliminary general remarks, I have had to take examples from the lowland area. (For the present purpose the exact position of the sites does not matter.) The eighteenth-century causeways tend also to be flatter than the Roman ones, which usually have a somewhat high camber. The metalled surface of a Roman road, when cleared of vegetation, is bounded by a setting of larger stones on either side, with usually a central rib as well. Both these features can be seen on Plate IV, which is from a photograph taken by the author of a portion of Roman road at Collielaw near Lanark, uncovered by Mr Davidson by whose kind permission it is here reproduced. You will see that the surface is much the same as that of the ordinary country roads before motors.

Ploughing destroys the metalled surface, but not the stones of which it is formed; it merely distributes them over a wider area. Perhaps a few of the bigger curbstones may be carried away by the ploughman to the side of the field, but the rest remain. It takes many decades of ploughing to level the causeway, and even then there remains a scattering of stones which from the air forms a belt of lighter colour along the line of the route, and which is often faintly visible even on the ground. The walker will, however, depend not so much on colour differences, though he does use them, as on the actual composition of the soil. He finds that, as one might expect, the line of the causeway across a ploughed field is quite perceptibly stonier, and it is even possible to record this photographically.

There is another soil-feature besides stoniness which helps one to trace the course of an obliterated causeway, and that is the presence of sandy grit. Sometimes this is very easy to see. It consists of the comminuted fragments of the road metal and is caused by horses' hoofs and cart-wheels. The same kind of grit is found to-day by the side of country roads; and before the main roads were made with asphalt it was a feature that every cyclist kept watch for. I think it would even be possible, by a soil analysis, to confirm the suspected course of a Roman road that had entirely vanished from ordinary observation. A comparison of soil samples from the site of the causeway and from elsewhere in the field should reveal a much larger pro-portion of sandy grit in the former. The test has never been made, but I hope some day it will be.

Of course when once a causeway has been ploughed, it loses its original appearance and the test of its edge-slopes, mentioned above, cannot be applied. In practice this test is often inapplicable, for one reason or another, and other criteria are more often used. To apply any of them one must walk along the road for a mile or two at least and study its general character and alignment. On open moorland an eighteenth-century road will be found to have culverts over small streams; and near the Beef-tub there are the remains of a stone bridge of modern character spanning a small ravine. On the other hand, when a Roman road comes to a stream nothing will be found except very occasionally the remains of an earthen ramp. The bridges, when they existed, were of wood; there are no remains of such in Scotland, so far as I know, but one was found and excavated in the fens of Cambridgeshire by Mr J. F. Kenny.[1] In the whole of Great Britain there is not one Roman bridge, except for the piers at Chesters on Hadrian's Wall; and all the many so-called 'Roman' bridges are of later date, usually of the eighteenth or nineteenth century. A causeway-road with culverts or bridges remaining may therefore be unhesitatingly dismissed as non-Roman. So too, a cause-way-road with hedges remaining must be ruled out, especially when the edge-slopes also give it away. Many such are still described as 'Roman roads' in local guide-books and elsewhere; and there were many on the

1 *Geogr. Journal*, LXXXII, 436–7.

Ordnance maps before I deleted them. But, easy as it may seem in some cases, there are pitfalls for the unwary in others. Take the example at Redshaw Burn near the Beef-tub.[1] Here we see on the upper left-hand part a Roman road which, in the middle, falls into and is overlaid by a fine eighteenth-century causeway-road. Both are typical examples of their kind, in almost mint condition. Just below the point of junction is a fine Roman fortlet. I had walked more than once along these two roads between the Beef-tub and Crawford—and so had one of my colleagues; it is one of the finest walks in Britain, both for scenery and loneliness. But, though we passed within a few feet of it, neither of us had seen the fortlet; and it was not until I was flying along the line of the Roman road in June 1939, on my way from Southampton to Lanark, that I discovered it. The banks of the fortlet are quite well preserved and easily seen on the ground. This is an example of air-discovery effected by means of the wider prospect one has from above. My chief purpose, however, in giving this illustration is to call attention to a pitfall. Here the eighteenth-century road-makers used and adapted the Roman causeway so long as it suited their purpose. The road they made would *appear* to be merely a modern one if one were content to examine only a small portion of it; it is not until one has walked its whole length that its composite nature is discovered, and I should add that I did discover this on the ground, before the air-photo was taken.

But the eighteenth-century roads had predecessors which were the merest cart-tracks. These, the only roads of medieval times, remained in use until they were superseded by something better in the eighteenth or nineteenth century. They are fundamentally different from, and inferior to, the causeway-roads which preceded and followed them: they have no causeway, and consist of one or more slightly sunken narrow tracks that wander over the moor, selecting the best gradients and avoiding peat-bogs. One such track near Elvanfoot has cut into the earlier Roman causeway but is in turn obliterated by the eighteenth-century causeway. At one place near the Beef-tub the causeways of the eighteenth-century and Roman roads are parallel to each other at a distance of 20 yards apart, while not far above them runs the medieval track. The old Selkirk-Peebles highway over Minchmoor is a track of this kind, barred at one point by a linear earthwork (Wallace's Trench).

These medieval tracks were not of course laid out or in any way aligned; they just grew. If they had makers it was the mules and pack-horses to

1 *Antiquity*, XIII (1939), p. 280, Plate II*b*.

whom the credit should be given. Mules are blamed for their obstinacy; but obstinacy is not necessarily a vice. It may be a virtue if the opinion held is correct; and in the selection of a route the opinion of a mule, who after all is an expert, is more likely to be correct than that of his rider. I once had an argument on this very point with a mule, and he convinced me by a practical demonstration that my view was wrong. The precise course followed by these moorland tracks is generally found to be the best possible selection from the various alternatives, which had all been tried in turn; it represents the survival of the one which, after many experiments, has proved fittest. Where the first road was a Roman one, that road would of course be followed so long as it remained in good condition. But when the wooden bridges broke down through neglect, the first divergence would be made; for the best place for a bridge is often not the best place for a ford, at any rate in hilly country. Other factors would cause other divergencies. Eventually a route would be established that, while following the same general course as the Roman road, would often be as much as a mile or more away from it. This reconstruction on *a priori* grounds agrees quite well with the observed facts.

There is one peculiarity I have noticed about the behaviour of Roman roads; they generally avoid narrow ravines, and they prefer not to go along the foot of very steep slopes. There are a few exceptions, as on the right (east) bank of the Clyde at Elvanfoot above Crawford where one of the two Roman roads here goes at the foot of Wellshoot Hill which rises 500 ft. above it and has a gradient of 1 in 3. Here there was no other course open to the road-makers. But below (north and west of) Crawford the Roman road avoids the narrow ravine of the Clyde above Abington and climbs, by a remarkable series of zigzags,[1] over the Raggengill Pass. I have little doubt that this avoidance was deliberate and for a purpose; whether so or not, it was because I anticipated it that I looked here for the Roman road, and found it. The road at Raggengill descends the north slope of the hill towards Abington; its appearance is old and smooth, unlike the sharp, fresh outlines of the eighteenth-century roads. The purpose of this avoidance of the Clyde gorge was probably tactical. Steep slopes and ravines are good places for an ambush, and for the rolling of rocks upon marching troops—a favourite device amongst all barbarians, and one also employed in Italy against the Black Shirt lorries in the earlier and bloodier days of that blood-stained

1 The only other example I know of is on Dere Street, south of the Roman camps and fortlet at Chew Green. See *Arch. Aeliana*, XIV (4th ser. 1937), p. 130.

episode, though I hasten to add that the rôles there were reversed. One such actual boulder, alleged to be 'stained with the blood of martyrs', was exhibited in the Fascist Exhibition in Rome in 1932, where I saw it.

A few words about the way in which air-photography reveals Roman sites and roads. In the course of this book I shall give some instances from our area, but the best, unfortunately, lie outside it. Such is Gallabury,[1] a small marching-camp in Lower Nithsdale, between Dumfries and Thornhill, which I discovered quite accidentally in 1939. The site was under grass and the soil a compact glacial sand, and a long drought had burnt the grass brown except over the levelled ditches where it had remained fresh and green, the silt of the ditches having retained more moisture. Exactly the same process showed up (near Lochmaben) the line of an already recorded but little-known Roman road, which stood out as a dead-straight band of parched brown grass traversing pastureland that was less parched.[2] Here the raised causeway had lost more moisture than the adjacent ground and the grass therefore withered more quickly. The road behaves in a rather curious fashion, making a very abrupt turn to avoid a lake visible in the foreground. Its course is, however, securely established. The Roman road near Gretna Green showed up from the air almost as plainly as the one just described, but on the ground, though plainly to be seen, it was less clear.

I have been obliged to select these examples from outside the region we are now to traverse, because there is none within it so apt to my purpose, which is to give you some idea of the nature of the remains we shall be studying there. Many of the places mentioned will no doubt be unfamiliar to you; but their position on the map is irrelevant for the moment. It is as examples or types that I have cited them. In the following pages I shall be dealing not so much with typology as with topography, and I shall endeavour to indicate the positions of sites by maps and diagrams, so far as I have been able to compose them under the very difficult circumstances of the present time. We are now ready to undertake our voyage of exploration into Roman Scotland starting at Camelon.

1 *Antiquity*, XIII (1939), p. 280, Plate v*a*.        2 Ibid. p. 280, Plate IV*b*.

# Chapter Two

## CAMELON TO ARDOCH

THE Roman fort of Camelon stands on a spur of high ground over-looking the estuary of the Carron, which must have been tidal before the dam was built at the Carron iron-foundry in the early eighteenth century. It lies about 2 miles west-north-west of Falkirk, in the angle between the Stirling and Glasgow roads, and close to the point where the main railway line divides, one branch going south-westwards to the Clyde, the other eastwards to Edinburgh. The fort actually stands midway between these two important road and railway junctions; and the geographical factors responsible for these modern divergencies must have influenced the choice of this particular site by Agricola in the first century. For reasons we shall see later, the only practicable route from the south into all that part of Scotland which lies north of the Forth must run between the trackless and barren Campsie-Gargunnock hills on the west and the Forth estuary on the east. The strip of land thus confined is about 10 miles long from Stirling to Camelon and increases in width from about 4 miles at Bannockburn to about 10 miles at the south end. But the effective width is considerably narrower on account of the impassable peat-bogs which still encumber the lowlands beside the Forth estuary, and which formerly were much more extensive. This corridor has been the scene of many battles, the chief of them Bannock-burn in 1314. It is thought probable by Professor Watson[1] that the hilly region on the west, which has now no all-inclusive name, is to be identified with the 'mons Bannauc' mentioned in the Life of St Cadoc who founded churches in this region and died about 570. (The name 'bannauc' means 'horned' and should refer to a district with many hill-peaks.) These uplands are almost devoid of habitations to-day, nor could I see any vestiges of ancient ones when I flew over them in 1939, save at one spot to be mentioned later.

In 1898 the site of the Roman fort at Camelon was selected for a foundry, and in the autumn the Society of Antiquaries was informed of the fact. There are two enclosures, called by the excavators the 'North Camp' and the 'South Camp'. The latter only was built over and the 'North Camp' is still open ground; when I was last there, in 1937, it was a cornfield. But instead

1 *Celtic Place-names of Scotland* (1927), p. 196.

of concentrating at once on the 'South Camp', which is now inaccessible, four or five months were allowed to slip by, and in March when excavation was at last begun, it was too late to do more than clear two groups of buildings in the 'South Camp'. Instead, the whole of the 'North Camp' was uncovered, and proved to be a fort of the Antonine period, whose plan shows the usual buildings—long rows of barracks, a buttressed barn, head-quarters building and Commandant's house (Fig. 1). For the history of the site, however, buildings in the 'South Camp' and certain ditches are of rather more importance, as Sir George Macdonald has shown. The buildings were numbered xv to xviii, and it is Nos. xvii and xviii that tell us most. No. xvii (Fig. 2) was a bath-building that had stood for some length of time, for buttresses had been added at a later date, and some additional rooms built on to the north-west corner. The buttresses 'indicate, not merely that the occupation with which No. xvii is to be associated was a long one, but also that it was secondary'[1] that is, that the bath-building stood not on the natural soil but on ground disturbed by an earlier occupation. Disturbance was, in fact, proved at the contemporary small building No. xvi, beneath which was found a deep pit and remains of another yet older building. The bath-house 'lay at a much lower level than the admittedly Antonine structures',[2] and Sir George assigns it to the Agricolan period.

Building No. xviii, which may have been the Commandant's house, was 'buried beneath a far larger accumulation of débris' than the buildings of the north, or Antonine, fort[3] and was therefore considerably earlier than this period. But its alignment is quite different from that of building No. xvii, also Agricolan. Thus we have evidence of *two* Agricolan occu-pations, one, represented by the bath-house (No. xvii), of considerable duration. The 'South Camp' was 'the chief source of the remarkable collection of relics, including much first-century Samian ware'. Thus the finds confirm the evidence of the buildings. Can we now associate the latter with any of the defences? Following Sir George Macdonald again (with additions of my own) I think we can. A ditch S was found, 19 ft. wide across the top, running north from the west gate of the 'South Camp'; at its north end it forms a rounded angle. I would suggest that this ditch continued southwards and was one of those parallel trenches which crossed obliquely the ditches at the south-west corner of the 'South Camp'.[4]

1 *J.R.S.* ix, 131.                                  2 Ibid. p. 130.
3 'The difference in level was sometimes as much as 8 feet' (p. 129).
4 *P.S.A.S.* xxxv, 366.

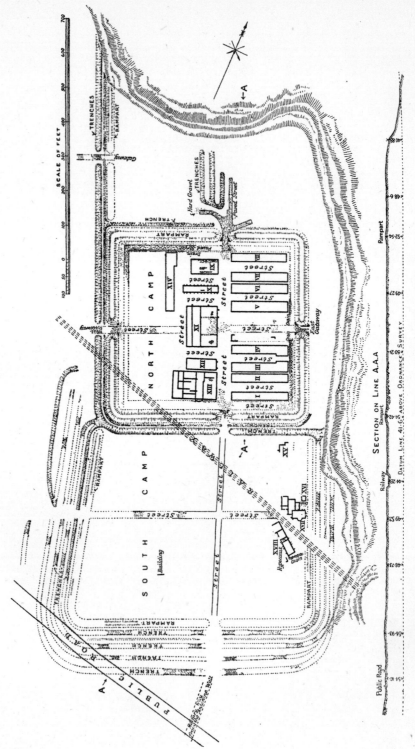

Fig. 1. Plan of Roman forts at Camelon.

'Differences in the filling' of these oblique trenches were noted as likely to prove 'of great assistance in distinguishing between them [and the ones they crossed], irrespective of difference in size and direction. The colour in this apparently older set was a warm brown throughout, and the soil was compact

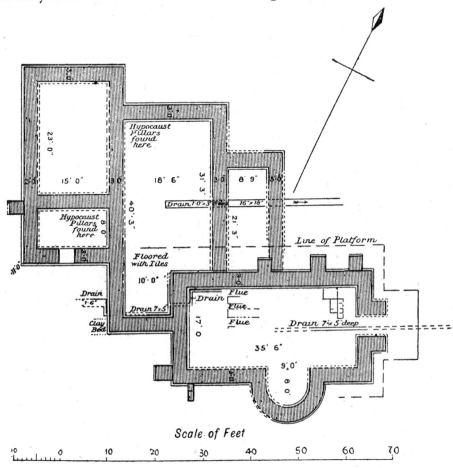

Fig. 2. Plan of building No. XVII at Camelon.

and contained few relics.' Unfortunately these valuable clues were not followed up. When we look for these older oblique trenches on the plan we do not find them! Instead we find an 'elaborate array of trenches' which is in fact largely conjectural and which Sir George regarded as 'prima facie suspicious'. The surveyor, 'in deference', Sir George says, 'to a weight of opinion which he was not in a position to resist'[1] was evidently not allowed

1 *J.R.S.* IX, 129.

to mar 'the homogeneous outline of the whole' by the insertion of these awkward intrusions. Yet they may have been the defences of one of the Agricolan forts, for, as Sir George points out, they seem to have been parallel to the alignment of building No. xvII, the bath-house, which is out of alignment with everything else. It should be added that at the time when he wrote his analysis of Camelon (about 1919), Sir George consulted the author of the 1899 excavation-plans, the late Mr Mungo Buchanan, who agreed that 'the entire plan of the ["South Camp"] must be set aside as untrustworthy, or, rather, as positively erroneous',[1] though I understand this to refer rather to the defences than to the buildings inside.

Can we go further and associate this north-west—south-easterly orientation with a hypothetical road coming from the south-east? It might well be the continuation of a road, whose existence is proved by a milestone, from Ingliston near Edinburgh; but no remains of it have been found.[2] I have always, however, suspected that some such road must have existed to connect with the northern end of the Roman road coming from Crawford and Biggar.

It only remains to say something about the three finger-like ditches outside the north gate of the 'North Camp'. Sir George wrote that 'a more thorough probing' might have 'revealed evidence of a reconstruction during the Antonine period'. From this admirably guarded statement I infer, entirely on my own responsibility, that the obvious resemblance to some gateways of Antonine forts did not escape the observation of their foremost excavator. The oblique line of ditch bounding their southern ends has parallels at wall-forts such as Mumrills and Castle Carey[3] and perhaps at Old Kilpatrick.[4] The 'paved street' running parallel with the three trenches, at a distance of about 12 ft. to the east of the edge of the innermost, may perhaps have been in reality the stone cradle of the rampart. The oblique line ceases at the gateway in the continuation of the west rampart of the 'North Camp', and a roadway was found there.

There was, therefore, a long and intensive occupation of Camelon during the Agricolan period, succeeded by an Antonine fort that may have been

1 *J.R.S.* IX, 129.
2 For the milestone (which is now in the Edinburgh Museum), see Robert Sibbald, *Historical Inquiries* (1707), pp. 41, 50; and Horsley, *Brit. Rom.* (1732), p. 203 (No. xxv) and references: for some seventeenth-century roads in Kirkliston, see *Analecta Scotica*, 1 (1834), No. xxIV, p. 54. I am indebted to Dr St Joseph for calling my attention to this milestone whose true character he was the first to recognise.
3 Macdonald, *Roman Wall in Scotland*, 2nd ed. pp. 196, 242.     4 Ibid. pp. 335, 336.

reconstructed. The general arrangement of the overlapping forts may be compared with that at Birrens and Mumrills. In view of these conclusions, and to verify them, it would be most interesting to excavate parts of the site again. Unless there have been changes since 1937, there still remains open and available nearly the whole of the 'North Camp' and the area north of it, and the north-east corner of the 'South Camp'. Building No. xviii was totally destroyed by 'railway operations';[1] but buildings Nos. xv, xvi and xvii, which lay south of the railway, may still be in existence, though partly covered perhaps by an earthen ramp leading to a foot-bridge over the railway.

'Camelon has been identified by Mr Richmond with Ptolemy's Lindum.[2] Watson explains the name as meaning 'pool' or 'lake',[3] equivalent to Welsh 'llyn', which fits the site admirably; for at the foot of the escarpment on north and east there are old marshy tracts, the former beds of the Carron, which must have been overflowed by the tide in Roman times.

'Camelon was the first site in Scotland where positive indications of the presence of Agricola were discovered', in the form of coins and early types of Samian ware.[4] It is appropriate therefore to choose Camelon as the starting-point of our much-delayed northern journey, since it seems likely that Agricola, whose footsteps we are to follow, started there too. But before finally setting out northwards along the road, we must cast one 'backward hurrying glance' to see whence it came. From the south gate of the southern fort at Camelon to the Antonine Wall is a distance of just half a mile; Roy[5] marks the road as running through the middle of both forts and as meeting the wall at an original gap in the wall protected by a guard-house. Here now stands a house called Watling Lodge, built in 1894 for a Mr Fairlie on the remains of an earthwork, probably a medieval castle-mound, which was lowered 6 ft. to accommodate it.[6] The course of the road is marked on the 6 in. map, but there are now no surface indications of it along this line, part of which is covered by the Camelon Chemical Works. The road itself, how-ever, is well authenticated, whatever may have been its exact course. It seems to have ended at the wall: no one has ever claimed that it continued directly southwards, the only road so doing of which there is any real evidence being that from the fort of Castle Carey, with which we are not

---

1 *P.S.A.S.* xxxv, 345.                     2 *P.S.A.S.* lvi, 292.
3 *Celtic Place-names*, p. 33.              4 *P.S.A.S.* lii (1918), p. 226.
5 *Military Antiquities*, Plate 29.
6 Macdonald, *Roman Wall in Scotland*, 2nd ed. pp. 344-7.

now concerned. Although I spent a whole day in 1937 looking for it without success, I still believe it exists and that it should be possible to replot its course on the map.

The excavators of Camelon marked a 'paved street' going north-westwards out of the gate in the north-west side of the northern fort; and General Roy also shows a road going out there and continuing to the edge of the cliff which it is shown descending, then across the low marshy ground and up the cliff on the other side. There are no traces of its presence to be seen on either of these cliffs, which the road would have negotiated by a sloping ramp, as elsewhere. Moreover, it was quite unnecessary to cross this low ground at all, since by going a little further west it could easily have been avoided. Nor is there any real reason to suppose it did. Already in 1777 Nimmo[1] could find 'scarce any vestige of it' between Camelon and the Carron, 'the fields having been in tillage from time immemorial'; if so, Roy can hardly have seen much of it only some twenty years before at the most.

Nimmo also records the discovery in 1773 of the alleged foundation-stones of a bridge, which he quite correctly suggests may have been remains of stone piers supporting a wooden structure. They were found 'by workmen, employed by the Carron Company to make a reservoir for the use of their works'. The dam of this reservoir is now marked 'weir' on the map; it is a quarter of a mile above Larbert Bridge and the materials were doubtless obtained from a quarry still indicated here on the south bank. The Ordnance map marks the site of the bridge; but since neither here nor at any point between Camelon and Stirling is there any concrete evidence to support the course of the road as marked on the Ordnance map, we may safely ignore it; I have examined the road's whole course on the ground and found nothing. That the Roman crossing was at the place where the foundations of the bridge-piers were found is the more likely because it was also the site of the ford in later times. Just north of it the name 'Castlehill' records the former existence of an artificial mound noticed by Gordon in 1727, where according to Macfarlane[2] was 'a batterie of cannon in defence of the bridge and ford when King Charles the Second his army lay in the muirs of Dunipace and Larbert 1651'. The mound was no doubt older, and the site of a medieval castle guarding the ford.

Nimmo continues: 'After the road hath got free of the river, it appears

1 *Hist. of Stirlingshire* (1777), p. 21.
2 *Geogr. Collections*, I, 331, sub anno 1723.

again upon a rising ground, a little westward of the church of Larbert, and holds a straight course by Torwoodhead, Drasyl, Plean-muir, Upper Bannockburn, the villages of Mill-town and St Ninians, and the town of Stirling.' I much regret that I did not come across this description in time to test it on the ground, but I have little doubt that it is in the main correct. Torwood Head is the name of a large house still standing on the west side of the Stirling road one and a half miles north-west of Larbert Church, at the south end of Torwood. 'Drasyl', spelt 'Drezeal' on his map, is now represented by the farms of North and South Durieshill. Near Torwood Head the Roman road must have left the line of the modern road and continued north-westwards through Torwood. In this very extensive old wood there is a broch called Tappoch on the edge of a precipice at the highest point in the wood, and at the south end there is a medieval castle. When I was there in May and June 1937, the wood was full of fallen conifers, around which for several years a dense growth of vegetation had entwined itself. It was as impassable as a tropical jungle, and not without its own special risks. I was all the more pleased therefore to be able both to locate and rule out the Ordnance map's course for the road, and to find another that seemed more likely. This other consists of a stony causeway in the north-west corner of the wood; it runs nearly parallel to the Ordnance course at a distance of about 400 ft. west of it, just inside the wood, whose western boundary is here followed by a small stream. I was able to trace the causeway southwards for over a quarter of a mile in a straight line; beyond this southwards the wood was impassable.

The best place to see it is where it is crossed by a footpath (not marked on the 6 in. map) 40 yards east of the western boundary of the wood, in the extreme north-west corner. I first found this in May 1937, but not being sure of it I revisited it again the next month. I still retain slight doubts about it, mainly on account of its width which seems too small for a Roman road; excavation would soon decide. The line, so far as I was able to plot it on the map, is an almost exact prolongation of the line of the modern road at East Plean Colliery, which by general agreement coincides with the Roman road. From this point I believe the two coincide more or less continuously for 4 miles to the outskirts of Stirling; but although I have examined the ground carefully I have not found any evidence of it. There is certainly no trace of it along the line indicated by the Ordnance map.

A writer in 1870, Miss Maclagan, has stated that 'immediately on the south side [of the broch] there still remains about a mile of the real Roman road. Its walls and ditches are most distinctly there.' This does not sound much like a Roman road, but the record is mentioned for what it may be worth.

At West Plean, on Common Hill, the Ordnance map marks what it calls a round 'fort'. I visited this in 1933 and found it to be a Roman signal-post of the type we shall encounter later on the Gask ridge, when I shall describe them more fully. It was seen soon afterwards by Sir George Macdonald[1] who wrote to me accepting it as such. It consists of a flat round table surrounded by a ditch with a low bank on the outside. The total or overall diameter is 40 yards. The hill was under permanent grass when I saw it, and the earthwork was in an excellent state of preservation; I hope it has not now been ploughed down. The hill is a little over 300 ft. high and commands a splendid view. The signal-post is 400 ft. south-west of the Roman road. Although I have looked for others like it along the road, I have failed to find any. The next one southwards might be on Greenhill, three-quarters of a mile to the south-east, from which point the top of Torwood is visible. There should be another in Torwood, and when the wood has been cut down and cleared it would be worth while searching there.

A mile north of the signal-post the Plean road joins the Glasgow road; the Roman road probably continued along the same alignment which would bring it into the Glasgow road at a bend a little further on; but there are no traces of it to be found there. Following the modern road we come to the ancient village of St Ninians, whose church and well[2] stood on the east side of the road. Then we come to the outskirts of the famous city of Stirling, the key of Scotland.

Stirling has almost every advantage that an ancient site required (Fig. 3). It stands on a tidal estuary, accessible to ships[3] but far enough from the open sea to be safe from piratical raids. It has a great impregnable wall with precipitous sides where the castle was built (and where before it a prehistoric fort must surely have been placed), and it commands the narrowest crossing-point of the flatlands of the Forth; from the foot of the Castle rock to the north side at Airthrey is only a mile. West of Stirling the Vale of Menteith widens out to 3 miles, and was moreover once covered by the huge peat-

1 See his *Roman Wall*, 2nd ed. (1934), p. 358.
2 *P.S.A.S.* XVII (1883), pp. 170–2 (plan of well).
3 For an interesting account, with documentation, of Stirling as a port, see *Trans. Stirling Nat. Hist. and Arch. Soc.* (1919–20), pp. 51–70: 'Early Navigation of the river Forth', by David B. Morris.

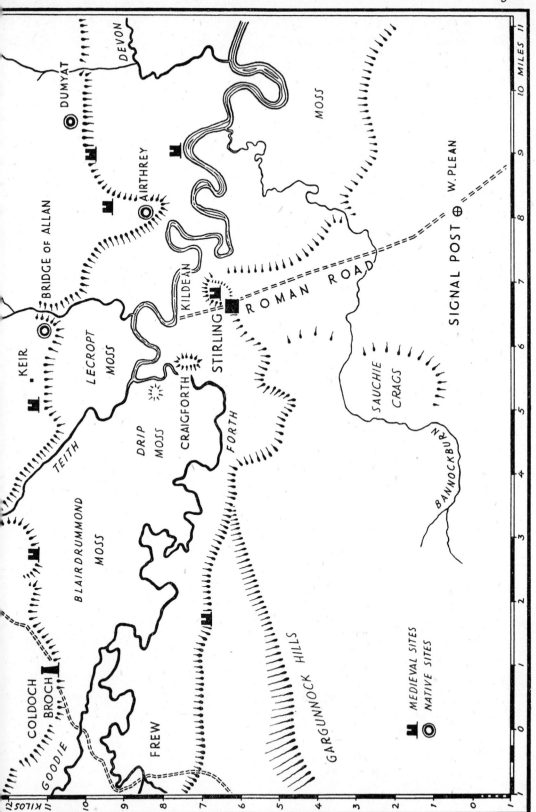

Fig. 3. The Vale of Menteith.

mosses of Lecropt, Drip, Blairdrummond and the still surviving mosses of Flanders, which extend right up to the foothills of the Highlands near Aberfoyle. Besides Stirling there were, before the clearance of the peat-mosses and the construction of modern roads, only two other ways across this wide vale: one passed round the west end, leading down over rough, hilly country to the Clyde; the other crossed the Goodie Water and the Forth between Flanders and Blairdrummond Mosses, where the vale is only 2 miles wide between the hard ground on either side. Between the western-most route and the western sea is an impassable tract of lofty mountains, and the western route is, apart from its own intractable nature, too far to the west to have served as a main thoroughfare of traffic; though it might have been of occasional use to raiding parties with a limited objective. Those travellers, whether bent on peace or war, who wished to pass from north to south Scotland, or vice versa, had therefore only two choices: one was to cross at Stirling and the other by the passage of the Forth and Goodie. This latter passage is used to-day by the road from Kippen on the south to Doune, by Coldoch. It passes four farms called Frew (North, Wester, Mid- and East Frew), and is to be identified with the famous Fords of Frew that were one of the Seven Wonders of Scotland. They are first mentioned inferentially in the Welsh Laws, when a Welsh raiding-party to the North disputed who should take the lead through the river Gweryd (Forth). In the Chronicle of the Kings of Scotland it is said that Kenneth (971–995) walled the banks of the ford of Forthin (? read Forthiu).

I must devote a little more space to the Fords of Frew because, although there is no evidence of their use in Roman times, they *may* have been in use then, and they are of outstanding historical importance as outflanking the crossing-place at Stirling. It is necessary to understand the topography of the Vale of Menteith. The peat-bogs rest upon a bed of carse-clay, an estuarine deposit laid down when the land stood lower and when this vale was an arm of the sea, as is proved by the discovery in the carse-clay of the bones of stranded whales. When the peat has been skinned off the top, the clay can be travelled over, though it must have been unpleasant going in wet weather. Between Flanders and Blairdrummond there was already in the eighteenth century a gap of about 3 miles—the Frew passage—where the peat had been removed. When was this gap formed? It is impossible to say precisely, but I think the beginning of the clearance of the peat may have begun early in the Christian era, if not before. Probably the first clearance was primarily for the purpose of obtaining fuel; perhaps not much clearance was actually required before a free passage across was obtained, for peat does not form on the banks of the rivers, and the road, be it noted, adheres as far as possible to river-banks in its winding course. Once the route was established, clearance would naturally proceed on either side of it until the gap was considerably widened. It may be significant that on the cliff at Coldoch, less than a mile east of the point where the road reaches firm ground at its northern end, is another of the rare southern brochs. Was it a robbers' castle on a much frequented route? There is another castle, of later date, at Kippen at the southern terminus.

Although important, from our present point of view, because it by-passed Stirling, the passage of the Fords of Frew was primarily a route leading from Dumbarton, the old British tribal stronghold, into northern Scotland by Strathallan and Strathmore.

No doubt it was from Dumbarton that the Welsh raiders referred to above set out. The Picts may have used the fords in their wars with the Scots. Dumbarton, indeed, may have derived some of its importance from the fact that it commanded the southern terminus of this route; it would thus have been the western equivalent of Stirling in some respects, though there could of course have been no bridge over the Clyde there. The old road may still be followed from Bonhill over Cameron Muir and by Killearn and Balfrons over Kippen Muir—and a pleasant one it is to walk along.

These geographical considerations are a necessary preliminary to the understanding of the importance of Stirling throughout early times. As I have said, we may be sure that the heights above the modern town must have been occupied in prehistoric times, and there is in fact a record of a hill-fort of unknown date on Gowan Hill, an open space north-east of the castle. It was described as a 'British round castle or mound now called "Murdoch's Know"'. Already in 1870 the vandals of the mid-nineteenth century had been at work, destroying it by the cutting of terraces, but it was still traceable. It seems to have consisted of a small inner area 50 ft. in diameter surrounded by two stone walls 25 ft. apart. It overhung and commanded the bridge of Stirling'.[1]

That the Romans must have occupied the site is on *a priori* grounds quite certain, as was long ago recognized, with characteristic insight, by Mr Ian Richmond.[2] Mr Richmond identified the unknown Roman fort he predicated here with the Coria of Ptolemy; the name, according to Watson,[3]

1 *P.S.A.S.* IX (1872), p. 34.                    2 *P.S.A.S.* LVI (1922), p. 296.
3 *Celtic Place-names* (1927), p. 32.

'probably means "hosting-place"; it would become in Gaelic *cuire*, which is common in Early and Middle Irish in the sense of "band, host"; "the battle of Cuire in Alba" is mentioned once at least in Irish literature'. The frequent occurrence of medieval battles round Stirling has already been mentioned, and the same topographical factors must have operated in earlier times. Mr Richmond's identification was made before Professor Watson's book was published, and its correctness is made even more probable by the fact, of which he does not seem then to have been aware, that the remains of a Roman fort at Stirling had actually been recorded. Speaking of 'the King's Knock or Mount', Maitland[1] says that the Roman road coming from the south 'joins the Roman station, on the southern side of the Castle, which is fortified with a rampart and a spacious ditch; which, though greatly defaced, appears to be of Roman construction'. The destruction of the Roman fort he attributes 'to the erection of a beautiful work, situated in the praetorium of the station, denominated the King's Knock or mount, for which the ramparts, and other fences belonging to the said praetorium, were obliged to make way'. He refers to the Roman fort as a 'large station'. The King's Knot is still there, and consists of an octagonal mound and a formal garden, laid out in 1627;[2] but that there was some earthwork there before is plainly suggested by Barbour's reference to a 'round table below the castle' in the fourteenth century.[3] William of Worcester (1415–82?) states that King Arthur 'custodiebat le round-table in Castro de Styrlyng, aliter, Snowdon west castell'.[4] The expression 'west castell' would only be intelligible if there were another fortification here, distinct from the castle on the rock and lying (as the Knot does) to the west of it. These passages suggest some round earthwork (perhaps a castle mound) standing within a Roman fort—compare the name 'Arthur's Round Table' for the sacred circle at Penrith. Before being aware of either these references or Mr Richmond's, I had been over the ground myself looking for Roman remains which I, too, had hoped to find there; but except for an enigmatic ditch I found nothing. Later, after finding Maitland's reference, I examined the site from the air with Mr Alington, whose photograph does not help much, though it does show certain marks. A few trial trenches would probably settle the matter.

1 *History of Scotland* (1757), p. 194.
2 *Arch. Journ.* XCIII, 315.
3 Nimmo's *History of Stirlingshire*, 3rd ed. 1 (1880), p. 82.
4 *Itin.* p. 311, quoted in Chalmers, 1, 245.

The name should be King's Knot (not Knock); the word 'knot' has as one of its meanings 'a flower-bed laid out in an intricate design; any laid out garden plot' (*O.E.D.*). Doubtless Maitland confused it with the Gaelic *cnoc*, a hillock. The existence of a mound here before the 'knot' or formal garden was laid out was demonstrated nearly 40 years ago by Mr W. B. Cook in his account of 'The King's Park of Stirling in history and record', published in a periodical[1] that is inaccessible in the south of England, but which contains much valuable matter relating to Stirling. The preceding paragraph, which comes to a similar conclusion, was written before I had been able to consult these *Transactions*.

I was hardly more successful in my search for the road.

There is a line of wall, separating two enclosures, at the back (west) of Randolphsfield, on the highest ground between the site of the fort and St Ninians; it is exactly 100 yards west of the west wall of the house of Randolphsfield. Here is a bank that looks rather like the causeway of a Roman road, and is worth uncovering; but I would not like to place too much reliance upon it. (This is in close alignment with the modern road through St Ninians, which, as we have seen, probably coincides with the Roman road.) There is nothing to be seen along the course marked upon the Ordnance map.

After writing the preceding paragraph I found that the Roman road had been reported along what appears to be the Ordnance map line (Fig. 4). Before 1907 it was 'uncovered at Laurelhill Place, while the house No. 27 Snowdon Place was being erected. It has also been seen on the other side of Snowdon Place at Nos. 18 and 20, and at 19 Park Terrace.'[2] These three spots do not actually fall into line with any of the three possible courses indicated; but a prolongation of the main road through St Ninians, from the cross-roads at the new church, where Bannockburn road comes in, to Bellfield road on the north, would almost coincide with the Randolphsfield bank and would pass through Nos. 18, 20 and 27 Snowdon Place and within a few feet of No. 19 Park Terrace. A very slight change of direction at the highest point (see diagram) would bring it through No. 19 as well. This St Ninians

1 *Trans. Stirling Nat. Hist. and Arch. Soc.* (1906–7), pp. 110–36; see also ibid. (1912–13), pp. 77–84, for the connotation of 'knot', and (1888–9), pp. 32–43, for the history of the King's Knot.
2 Ibid. (1907–8), p. 49. I have to thank the Burgh Engineer of Stirling, Mr David B. Marrs, for kindly identifying these numbers for me. The plan reproduced on p. 24 is based on a tracing of the 25-in. O.S. map supplied by him.

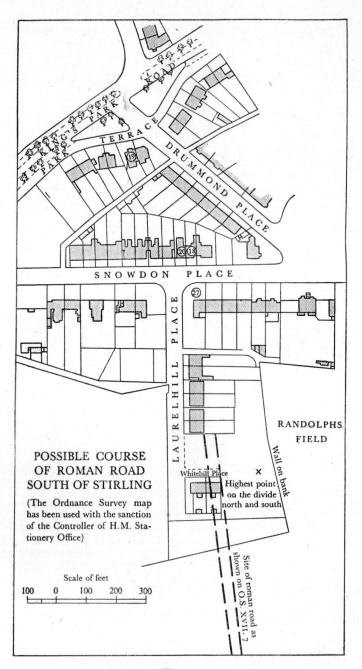

POSSIBLE COURSE
OF ROMAN ROAD
SOUTH OF STIRLING

(The Ordnance Survey map
has been used with the sanction
of the Controller of H.M. Sta-
tionery Office)

Scale of feet

100    0    100    200    300

Fig. 4.

line is continued northwards by Victoria Place (at the top of the plan opposite), whose western side has no houses but is bounded by an iron fence (or was in 1937). The ground inside (west of) the fence is grass-grown, and immediately beside the fence I noticed in 1937 the remains of a stony bank or causeway. It had seats on it. This may be the Roman road; but we must allow for the possibility of its representing the remains of an old park pale.

The Roman fort guarded the crossing of the Forth, one of the most critical points in its whole course. Exactly where that crossing was is uncertain, and Nimmo's account is inconsistent.

He seems to think it crossed the Forth by the Ford of Drip, which not only involves an impossibly abrupt change of direction, but also a crossing of the much bigger Teith river immediately after—a crossing that is entirely unnecessary. He does hint, however, that it may have followed a sloping path called Ballochgeich[1] leading from the castle hill down to the river at Kildean; and he says that at Kildean 'very plain traces of it are discernible at a farmhouse, which, together with its offices and yards, is situated upon the very summit thereof'. Kildean is on the correct alignment, and there seems at some time to have been a ford there. In the early eighties of the last century Mr W. B. Cook, in a dry summer, walked dry-shod 'a good part of the way' across and observed 'some large flat stones mortared together...in the bed of the river'. He also records that 'Donald King, the miller at Kildean in the middle of the [nineteenth] century, told the late Mr James Lucas, writer, that...he recollected many of the stones being taken out for the purpose of repairing the piers on each side of the river. [These were not bridge-piers, but to protect the banks from erosion by the current.]...Several of them were so firmly built into the bed of the river that it was impossible to raise them. These are no doubt the stones I saw...they are clearly the pavement of the ford and...I should not be surprised if these stones turn out to be part of the Roman road.'[2] That the Roman crossing was somewhere hereabouts I feel convinced, for several reasons. From the foot of the castle hill to the

1 Gaelic *Bealach-(na-)gaig*, 'pass of the cleft', an exact description of the path which descends by a narrow cleft. The Roman road can never have gone through this cleft, which, however, may well have been used in medieval times as a path to the ford at Kildean.

2 *Trans. Stirling Nat. Hist. and Arch. Soc.* (1904–5). Mr Cook argues strongly and convincingly in favour of the antiquity of Stirling Bridge, which Mr W. L. Shirra believed to have been originally at Kildean where accordingly he would locate the famous battle of 1297. Mr Cook's views received confirmation by the discovery of two stone piers of an older bridge 65–75 yards above the medieval bridge of Stirling (*Trans.* [1905–6], pp. 33–5, with plan). Mr Shirra's views are stated at length in the *Transactions* (1907–8), pp. 38–65.

hard ground at Cornton across the Forth is well under a mile—a shorter distance across even than the short medieval and modern one by Stirling Bridge. A crossing further west would lead to the huge impassable Moss of Lecropt, a mile wide, or to the Teith; while a crossing lower down is topographically impossible. But what happened to the road when it had crossed the Forth no one knows. Nimmo confines himself to the statement that it reappeared at Dunblane, but he gives no particulars. No one else has recorded any but the most general statements of its course between here and Ardoch, and I believe that no one has ever seen any remains of it. In 1937 I spent several days in the district examining the country between Stirling and Dunblane with only negative results, as far as the Roman road was concerned.

I do not therefore propose to waste any space recounting the various hypotheses upon which I worked since they all proved untenable—or at any rate unproven. The time in the field was not wasted—it never is, for one gets to know the country in a way that only exploration on foot can make possible, and one makes minor discoveries. I found two unrecorded round cairns, and satisfied myself that the 'supposed Roman camp' on Gallow Hill was in fact a native fort. I also traced the course of the two old roads, one on each side of Allan Water, that led southwards from Dunblane to Stirling.

It has generally been thought that the straight modern road between Dunblane and Greenloaning—the main north road—is of Roman origin, and I admit having rather reluctantly marked it as doubtfully Roman on the map. At the time I did so there was no evidence against it. Since then, however, in 1939, the road has been dug into to some depth in several places and no trace whatever has been found of anything that could be regarded as a Roman road. I am indebted to Mr Angus Graham for this information. The date when this road was constructed here is not known to me; Maitland in 1757 described it[1] as 'the new road lately made by the Government, leading by the town of Crieff, through the Highlands, to the town of Inverness'. There are several other long and straight stretches on this road, one of which—between Ardoch and Muthill—is demonstrably non-Roman, for it diverges from the known Roman road at an acute angle. Before 1939 one might have argued that the eighteenth-century road-makers used an existing Roman causeway as the foundation of their own road, but one can do so no longer.

[1] *History of Scotland*, p. 195.

It might be of some help if one knew the route followed by the pre-eighteenth-century road along Strathallan, but I have not been able to discover this. There is an old causeway-road over Sheriffmuir between Gathering Stone and Head Dyke, but it is of eighteenth-century type.

So we come to Greenloaning on the outskirts of the great Roman site at Ardoch (which I must leave for the next chapter). But first there are a few jokers to dispose of. I call them 'jokers' but the last laugh may well be upon me; I hope it will.

The first two are inscriptions. One of them is a large flat stone discreetly hidden behind a bush outside the Smith Institute at Stirling. It was found (on the farm of Townhead) in 1822 at a spot called the Roundel, five-eighths of a mile south-west of Greenloaning station. The Roundel is a round cairn, 100 yards in circumference and about 5 or 6 ft. high, round whose edge are planted seventeen beeches. There are many small boulders visible, but no central cist or peristalith of curbstones. The field was under grass in 1936 but showed evident signs of former arable. The inscription struck me as a forgery the moment I saw it. The letters are sharply cut with narrow lines, though it is only fair to say that one of the former farm hands admitted having rechiselled them. The published photograph shows fugitive traces of other letters; and it was said at the time of its discovery that one line read

VERSAMEBONOTVO

which may be translated 'turn me over for your own good'. I have not done so, as it seems unnecessary.

The other joker goes back to Sibbald (1641–1722). Miss Maclagan[1] described the rock on which this inscription is carved as 'on the brow of the hill' (i.e. Gowan Hill) 'facing the west'; and the rock itself as 'in form more like a garden bench than anything else, the letters being, as it were, upon the seat'. She thought she could distinguish the letters of the inscription and enclosed a tracing to the Society with her letter to the Secretary. The letter was published, but not her reading of the inscription. Some letters, D.F., seemed to be of a different date. Sibbald[2] merely says it was 'on a rock below the Castle' and that his copyist read it

IN EXCV. AGIT. LEG. II

1 *P.S.A.S.* IX (1872), pp. 178–9.
2 *Historical Inquiries* (1707), p. 35. In Nimmo's *History of Stirlingshire*, 3rd ed. I (1880), p. 16, it is described as 'upon a rock opposite to the old gate of the castle' and 'now obliterated'.

Horsley gives much the same transcription but identified it with another, reading

DE

IXIEX COTH AYIS

DI LET ALM

RE

adding that 'some suppose it to be in the *Highland* tongue'. We may safely leave it at that. The inscription was still to be seen, with difficulty, ten years ago when an unsatisfactory photograph of a cast in the Smith Institute, Stirling, was published, together with a description of it.[1]

The third is near Callander. Here two sites have been claimed as Roman, one west of the village and the other east. The western one is at a farm called Bochastle, first mentioned in Macfarlane's *Geographical Collections*;[2] in 1724 Alexander Graham of Duchray called it 'Mochaster or the Castle field' and recorded that a gold coin of Nero had been found near it recently; but he gave no description except that it was a 'camp'. Chalmers[3] seems to have derived his information from the *Old Statistical Account* and Stobie's Map of Perthshire, where the camp is marked by a purely conventional rectangle. The site seemed a likely one for a Roman fort, situated as it is at one of the gates of the Highlands, as Chalmers himself, anticipating Mr Richmond by 130 years, acutely perceived—indeed, he does actually mention the other two at Dalginross and Comrie. For these reasons I decided to make a special journey there in the middle of November 1938. The sun was kind and emerged for just long enough to enable me to photograph the bank of the supposed camp. At first I thought I had really discovered—or rather redis-covered—a Roman marching-camp; had I done so I should no doubt have been told that it was already well known, for had not Stobie marked it and others described it long ago? But surely these sites must be re-viewed in the light of present knowledge before they can be accepted; and the re-viewer has after all some claims to merit. Alas, the bank seems hardly massive enough even for a Roman marching-camp, much less for a fort; though the present width (12 ft.) is almost adequate for the former. A length of about 100 yards of it is preserved, forming the north bank of the farm enclosure; it might well have been also the yard-bank of a medieval castle, represented by the ruins of a round building. Beside this on the east is a long, single-storied, slate-roofed

1 *Trans. Stirling Nat. Hist. and Arch. Soc.* (1934–5), pp. 71–4.
2 I, 336.　　　　　　3 *Caledonia*, I (1807), p. 172, note o.

building—the old farm-house, now used as a stable; and north-east of it stands the present farm-house, built in the nineteenth century. There was something here in 1452 when it was called Mochastir. The name, according to Watson, means 'hut (*both*) of the castle', and may be evidence of something still earlier there. In spite of appearances I still have hopes that excavation may reveal a Roman fort; the spot is so eminently suitable, both topographically and strategically.

The site on the east of Callander was first mentioned in 1723 by an anonymous writer in Macfarlane's collections,[1] who refers to 'the vestige of a camp, but by whom framed is uncertain, a litle space be east the church upon both the side of the river of Teith'. The last remark arouses suspicion at once. Not even a marching-camp can have had a river as big as the Teith flowing through the middle of it. Alexander Graham in his account of 1724[2] says it was 'a quarter of a mile below the church on the north side of the said water', and that it was called 'Ball-Anton or the town of Antonius'. I did not know of this site when I went there, but from the map the alleged remains would appear to be glacial mounds.

I fear this chapter has been rather a dreary catalogue of blanks; but in that it reflects the common experience of field investigators. One has to reject as spurious or irrelevant the majority of sites one visits on the ground; from the air it is otherwise. It is only the inexperienced who make startling discoveries on every outing. We have at any rate cleared the way to Ardoch, one of the major Roman sites, which I shall describe in the next chapter.

1 *Geogr. Collections*, I, 134: another description on p. 336.　　　2 Ibid. I, 336.

# Chapter Three

## ARDOCH TO STRAGEATH, WITH DIVERSIONS

WE left the Roman road hanging in the air somewhere between Dunblane and Ardoch, having perforce had to abandon the hypothesis that the straight modern highway represents it. That straight section of 4 miles ends at Greenloaning, a small hamlet standing at the point where the road divides, one branch going to Perth and Aberdeen, the other to Crieff and Inverness. The fort of Ardoch stands on the east side of the Crieff road which has cut into the western defences of the fort as it climbs the hill after crossing the river Knaik. It was while crossing the park of Ardoch south of the fort that I happened to notice the rounded hump of a Roman causeway, low, broad and grass-grown but unmistakable. I first followed it northwards. It climbs the southern slope of Chapel Hill as a terrace, 6 yards wide, curving right up to the south gate of the fort. At the foot of the slope it begins its direct southern course, crossing the Knaik obliquely immediately above the disused bridge of Ardoch drive. The hump of the causeway is plainly visible in the trees south-east of the drive south of the bridge, where too an old river-terrace comes in from the south. For 200 yards southwards from the trees the causeway is plainly visible; then it encounters some ancient remains of unknown age, probably post-Roman, consisting of an earthen circle 35 yards across, a rectangular enclosure about $130 \times 100$ ft., both on the east side of the road, and a mound on the west, midway between the circle and the lodge. Beyond these the causeway is again visible, continuing in the same alignment for another 200 yards to a point just outside the park where it changes direction very slightly towards the west of south. It goes on for 300 yards in this direction till it enters the plantation on the east side of the Crieff road north-east of the tenth milestone from Crieff, where it is lost. Although I searched everywhere for it on this alignment near Greenloaning I could find no traces of it. The total length thus discovered is just under a mile. The northern portion aims directly at a natural knoll at Greenloaning marked by a clump of beeches, an ideal site for a signal-post, but I could find no trace of such. From this knoll Ardoch is visible $1\frac{1}{2}$ miles to the north, and there is a fine view also south-westwards.

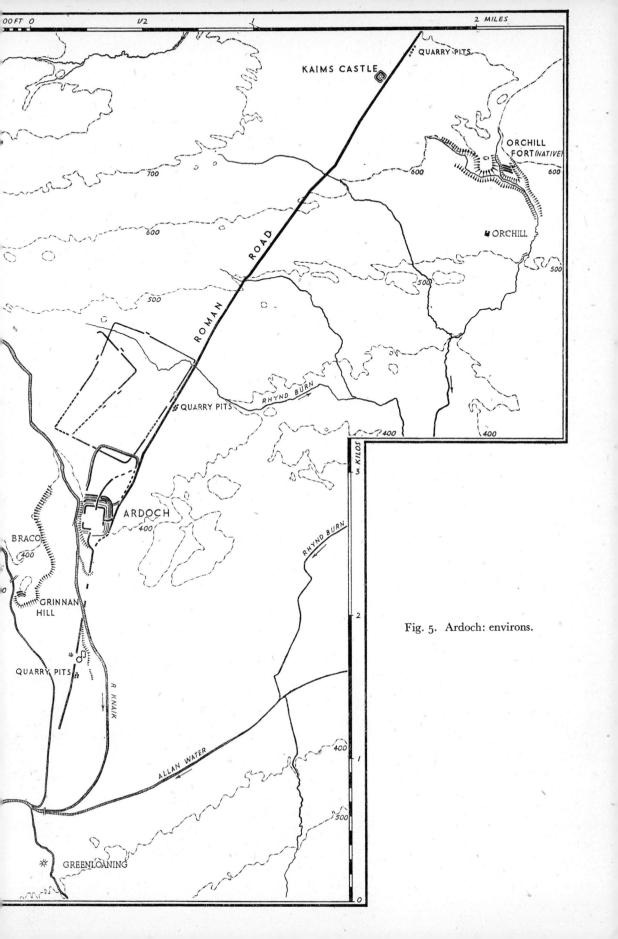

Fig. 5. Ardoch: environs.

I discovered this road in June 1937, in the course of a three days' examination of Ardoch fort and its environs. At that time I did not know that any previous investigators had seen it. When rereading the account of the Ardoch excavations I found that Maitland had already described it in general terms; his words are: 'Crossing the riveret Allan, near the wood-end, [it] goes on and crosseth both the new road and the water of Kneck a little below the bridge; and ascending the eminence, runs along the eastern side of the Roman camp, near the village of Ardoch.'[1] In the Ardoch report, Dr Christison quoted this passage (incorrectly), and stated that 'Maitland appears to be the only authority who professes to trace the military way south of Ardoch towards the Antonine Vallum'.[2] Dr Christison himself maintained a discreet silence on the subject; one infers that he never detected the road himself during his twelve months' study of the earthworks there, and also that he rather doubted whether Maitland, or his informant, had seen it either. But then Dr Christison held curious views about these 'military ways', as he calls them. He saw 'nothing extravagant' in the supposition that they were made, not by the Romans but by the Caledonian barbarians they were fighting.[3] And he even considered it necessary, when describing the defences of the fort itself, to discuss 'whether this unique design could have emanated from Roman engineers', concluding that, 'on structural grounds' there was 'no insuperable difficulty' in assuming this![4]

The Roman remains at Ardoch consist of two groups of earthworks, those represented by the ramparts of the superimposed forts, and those of the camps outside on the north. These latter being unquestionably the earlier we shall deal with them first. There is a large marching-camp, a smaller one, an enclosure called the 'procestrium', and a signal-post.[5] I have not examined the marching-camps closely on the ground, and shall therefore say no more than that they are for the most part levelled, though fragments survive in woods in the neighbourhood of Black Hill. On the east side of the larger camp are the remains of a signal-post of the large or Kaims Castle type (but half its size); it was first recorded by Roy, and later planned by Mr Richmond who has shown[6] that the bank of the camp has cut through the east side of the signal-post (Fig. 6). There is an entrance of the camp

1 *History of Scotland*, I (1757), p. 195.        2 *P.S.A.S.* XXXII (1898), p. 427.
3 Ibid. p. 435.                                    4 Ibid, p. 421.
5 Pennant claims to have seen part of a third marching-camp and marks it on his plan: *A Tour in Scotland* (1776), Pl. II, p. 103, plan facing p. 101.
6 *Arch. Journ.* XCIII (1937), p. 314.

at this point which, owing to its proximity to the Roman road, has no traverse, the ramparts being instead made to overlap. These facts have useful bearings on the relative age of the objects concerned. Moreover Roy observed that the defences of the smaller marching-camp cut through those of the larger and were therefore later. We thus get the following sequence: (1) road and signal-post, (2) large marching-camp, (3) small marching-camp. Roy also observed, and it is still plainly to be seen, that the north defences of the 'procestrium' cut through and are later than those of the

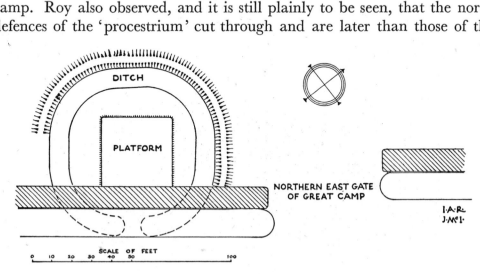

Fig. 6. Signal-post, Ardoch.

large marching-camp. There are no points of contact between the 'procestrium' and the smaller camp, so that on these grounds there is no evidence to show which was the older. But I suggest that the so-called 'procestrium' was in fact a labour-camp,[1] like that at Chew Green; if so, it must have been made to contain the builders of one of the forts, whose escort may have occupied the smaller marching-camp.[2]

There is a close parallel between the works at Chew Green[3] and those at Ardoch, down even to the purely fortuitous presence of a medieval chapel in each. At both sites there were two marching-camps, one large and one small,

[1] I put this suggestion to Mr Richmond in conversation, and he regarded it as a possibility that was worth consideration.
[2] The relations between the east bank of the 'procestrium' and the Roman road are obscure. It would appear to impinge closely upon the road. Excavation is needed to clear up this point.
[3] See Mr Richmond's excavations, published in *Arch. Aeliana*, xiv (4th series, 1937), pp. 129–50 and his summary in the *Hist. of Northumberland*, xv (1940), pp. 75–6, where the very fine air-photograph is published, facing p. 76.

labour-camps (if I am right) with stronger defences, and a fort that was remodelled more than once. But the works at Ardoch, though proportionate in size, are all much bigger than those at Chew Green.

'Ardoch', said Sir George Macdonald,[1] 'remains in its decay more impressive than any other Roman fort in Scotland.' That, however, is only because there the decay is less advanced than on the other sites where the farmer and nineteenth-century 'improver' and 'developer' have levelled the defences. The fort, which we will now consider, presents a bewildering maze of banks and ditches whose disentanglement is a fascinating exercise in logic. It was excavated by the Society of Antiquaries in 1896–7 under the direction

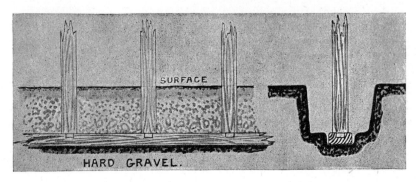

Fig. 7. Ardoch: sections of sleeper-trench.

of Mr J. H. Cunningham, whose report[2] records 'a very remarkable achievement, unrivalled in its day'[3] and one for which 'no praise can be too high'.[4] His outstanding merit is that he recognized, followed up and recorded on his plan, the post-holes first detected by his Clerk of the Works, who is illustrated in the Report[5] but remains, like so many pioneers of technique, anonymous. There were, in fact, two kinds of 'hole'—those for posts and those for sleepers. The round post-holes were of course for the uprights of timber buildings. Besides these were found the trenches occupied by wooden sleepers in which the uprights had been set (Fig. 7). Sir George has pointed out that these two different methods reveal on the plan two corresponding systems of different ages, 'or more probably three'.[6] 'The wooden buildings evidently belonged to a period when the enclosure was rather larger than it is now. A glance at the plan will show that in the north-east quarter, which alone was thoroughly cleared out, the post-holes and sleeper-tracks approach the

1 P.S.A.S. LII, 230.                           2 P.S.A.S. XXXII (1898), pp. 436–71.
3 Richmond, Arch. Journ. XCIII, 314.          4 Sir George Macdonald, J.R.S. IX, 122.
5 P. 441.                                       6 P. 126.

rampart so closely that they almost seem to impinge upon it. They certainly leave no room for the *intervallum*'[1] (Fig. 8). With the destruction of one or other of these groups of wooden huts I would associate the extensive layers of charcoal several inches thick which were encountered; and I would further point out that the presence of this charcoal layer on both the so-called 'ravelins' to the north of the inner rampart proves, if my suggested explanation of them is correct, just such an extension as Sir George demanded on other grounds and in another (easterly) direction. The charcoal layer is older than the middle (earlier Antonine) rampart which partly overlaps it, and it had already been buried under 3 ft. of débris when the (later Antonine) obliquely-set trenches were dug through it (see Plate VI of the Report, Section 1).

After these two, or three, 'wooden' periods came what Sir George calls the 'stone age' of the fort, represented by a long narrow building whose foundations were just below the present surface and some distance above the wooden holes. This Sir George regards as a *centuria* and, with others that left only occasional traces, as 'contemporaneous with the defences in their latest form—that is, with the defences as we know them now'.[2] The finds indicate occupation during both the Agricolan and Antonine periods, and we may associate the stone buildings with the later Antonine and the two or three periods of wooden buildings with the Agricolan.

Can we associate these occupations with the defences? Only to a limited extent without further excavation. The latest, and therefore Antonine, stage is represented by the inner rampart. Note that there is an entrance causeway across the ditch in the middle of the north side of this rampart and that similar causeways intercept the other ditches on this side of the outer rampart (whose ditch was not discovered). Excavation proved that originally only the ditch of the inner rampart, of the next (obliquely set) ditch[3] and the outermost one had causeways and that the two ditches in front of the middle rampart were continuous and unbroken. Obviously they must have been filled in when this entrance, belonging to the latest phase, was in use. Equally obviously they must belong to an earlier phase (represented by the middle rampart) which had no north gate. The plan plainly suggests that this middle rampart, with its ditches, represents an earlier form of the fort,

---

1 Sir George Macdonald, *J.R.S.* IX, 124.        2 Ibid.

3 Note also that the causeway-gap of this ditch is *in line with* the gaps north and south of it, and with them forms part of a single, obliquely-set line of approach to the inner fort, and made at the same time. From this it must follow that both the oblique trenches and the outer rampart are later than the larger (earlier) fort—a fact obvious also from the plan.

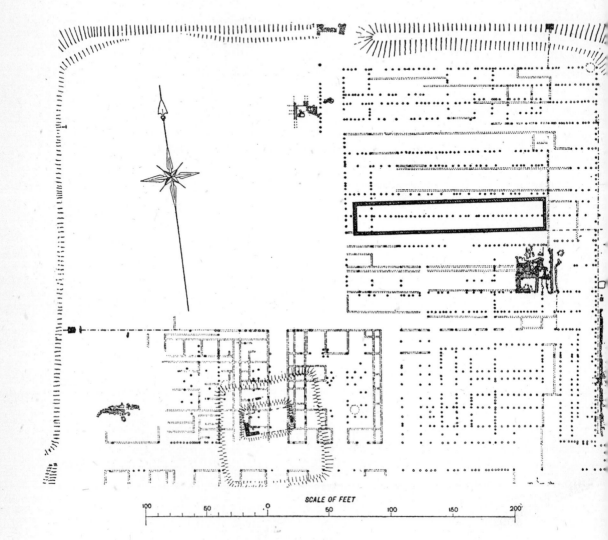

SCALE OF FEET

Fig. 8. Interior of Ardoch Fort: excavated portion.

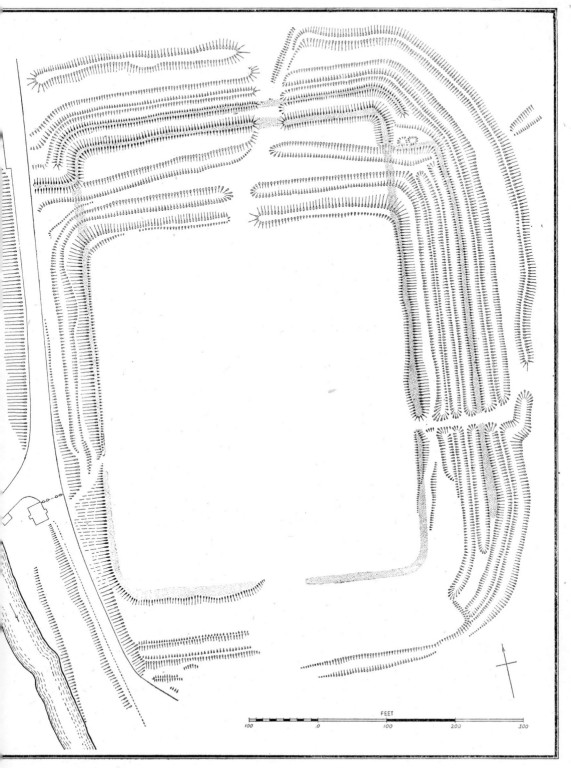

Fig. 9. Ardoch: the forts. The faint stipple indicates the outline of the conjectural early fort.

of the same breadth, but longer north and south. In fact the ditch of the middle rampart was found between the two areas at the north-west corner (see Plate VI of the Report, Section 8).

This last phase but one, therefore, consisted of an oblong fort whose north side ran parallel to the later north rampart, at some distance to the north of it, its east and west sides coinciding with the east and west walls of the later fort (Fig. 9, stipple). But we cannot associate this larger fort with the wooden buildings since it gives us no more room for them in the east than does the later fort. We thus have, probably, two stages within the Antonine period, in the earlier of which there was no north entrance.

When seen in section, the inner rampart differs in composition from the others and appears to have been reconstructed. Such reconstruction must surely belong to the last phase of all, for the rampart can hardly have existed at all in any form during any of the preceding periods. Between it and its ditch were observed the remains of another and smaller ditch, belonging perhaps to an earlier stage.

No defences that can be associated with the Agricolan wooden buildings can be disentangled. This is the task of the next excavator who must assuredly come forward before long; and I hope it will be Mr Richmond.

Before leaving Ardoch I must say a word about its name. The word 'Ardoch' means 'high place', consisting of the Gaelic adjective *ard*, high, with the suffix -*ach*, equivalent to -*iacum* so common in Old Gaulish place-names. But the old Gaelic name of the fort was Cathair Mhaothail, according to Watson,[1] a name surviving in that of the adjacent village of Muthill, in whose parochial area the fort stood. The word 'cathair' is connected with Latin 'cathedra' meaning a seat or principal residence, as in the name 'Arthur's Seat'; it is applied to hill-forts, as in the two Catherthuns in Angus, and occurs almost exclusively in the east of Scotland.

Professor Watson[2] suggests that this distribution of 'cathair' is additional evidence of an early infiltration from Munster where the name is very common. These early Gaelic-speaking settlers seem to have called their new home 'Eriu', a name surviving in Strathearn, the Vale of Eriu (gen. Erenn) or Ireland. Perhaps the same name occurs in the farm and burn of Rottearns, Greenloaning, which Watson identifies with the Rath Erenn of old writers— Ireland's rath or fort. It was the home of St Fillan. There is now nothing ancient to be seen at Rottearns; but it is only just over a mile from the fort of Ardoch, and one might ask whether the name might not have been taken

1 *Celtic Place-names*, p. 223.              2 Ibid. p. 222.

from that fort. It is not uncommon for such a transference of a name from an abandoned site to the nearest inhabited place. If so Rath Erenn would have been an alternative name for Ardoch. The evidence for this very interesting early Irish infiltration has been summarized in the introduction to the Ordnance Survey Map of Britain in the Dark Ages (North Sheet), whose debt to Professor Watson's work is there acknowledged.

The Roman name of the fort was probably Alauna. This name is mentioned by Ptolemy and the identification is Richmond's.[1] The name is a common one for rivers, and means rocky. The river Allan which flows past Green-loaning represents an early Alauna, thus supporting the identification.

The village of Ardoch is called Braco. On a spur of land close-by called Grinnan Hill, between the Knaik and the Keir Burn, is a small native promontory fort. It is called 'Roman fort' on the Ordnance map, but there is no evidence of Roman work there. It is said to be connected with the Roman fort by a secret passage containing vast treasure, commemorated in the rhyme

> From the camp of Ardoch
> To the Grinnin hill of Keir
> Are nine Kings' rents
> For seven hundred year.

But we must tear ourselves away from this fascinating spot and proceed on our way northwards along the Roman road to Strageath. The course of the road is marked continuously on the Ordnance map. I have walked along the whole of it once and over parts of it several times, in 1925, 1936, 1937 and 1940; and I flew over it in 1939. Except for short lengths the course marked is correct and can be verified by visible remains in many places.

The causeway can be traced without a break from Ardoch fort for over a mile. There are about half a dozen quarry-pits on the east side immediately south of Blackhill wood. The causeway was metalled with round pebbles which help identification. There is a slight change of direction to the east where it crosses a road from Gannocks to Dochlewan. It meets the Crieff road at the seventh milestone from Crieff, appears to coincide with it for 400 ft. where that road crosses a valley on an embankment, leaves the road on its west side at an old quarry and rejoins it at the north of the curve. It leaves the modern road again, as marked on the map on the west side, at Orchill Wood and can be seen quite plainly (as marked) running between the signal-post of Kaims Castle and the modern road. Where it coincides

1 *P.S.A.S.* LVI (1922), p. 296.

for 350 ft. with the modern road there is a row of quarry-pits on the east side that were seen and recognized as such by both Mr Pennant and Bishop Pococke in the eighteenth century.[1] Immediately north of these, in a bend in the modern road, on a piece of heather-moor, the causeway is very well preserved, being 24 ft. wide and 3 or 4 ft. high.

Three-quarters of a mile to the south-east of this point, on a spur of land 500 yards north-north-east of Orchill House, there is a native promontory-fort, excavated by Christison.[2] The site is not marked on the Ordnance map and was difficult to locate. I found it eventually however; it is marked by a single sycamore, and consists of three parallel ramparts facing north, the outermost being 150 ft. long from scarp to scarp. Inside and parallel to the ramparts Christison found two trenches with remains of a wooden palisade. Two miles east-south-east are the remains of another native fort (misnamed 'supposed Roman outpost' on the Ordnance map); it has been almost completely obliterated by the Gleneagles golf-course.

To resume our course. Beyond the point we left it, for a distance of just over a mile and a half, there are no certain traces visible of the causeway; but at two points there are what I took to be slight indications that the course is correctly marked on the map. After crossing the Machany Water, at Crosshill, the course marked is stony. There are possible traces in Culdees Park (a little to the south-east of the course marked) with a mound on the east side 800 ft. south of East Lodge. It leaves the park at the Lodge, and from there through Pirnhill Plantation it is very well preserved (23 ft. wide at the top and 27 ft. overall) for over half a mile, with quarry-pits on the west side immediately north of the Lodge. It is visible for 400 ft. on either side of the road from Dalpatrick to Auchterarder; in the field south-west of the road it appeared, in 1925 when the field was under plough, as a broad raised pebbly causeway; in 1940 the field was under grass and there was little to be seen. Close beside it in this field I observed in 1925 a stony mound about 25 yards in diameter. North of the modern road the causeway makes a sharp bend and enters the fort of Strageath.

The ramparts of the fort have been nearly levelled by cultivation which had begun in Roy's time, but with the help of his plan, of the air-photo (Plate V, taken during our flight in 1939), and repeated efforts on foot, it is possible to restore the main outlines. The sides of the fort are about 430 ft. in length. There is a gap visible in the west side, and there must have been another in the north side where a branch road (visible on the air-photo in

1 *P.S.A.S.* XXXII, 429.      2 *P.S.A.S.* XXXIV, 117, No. 47; XXXV, 22.

the next field) left it to join the main road. On the level ground west of the fort Roy's plan and the air-photo show a number of banks which cannot now be reduced to any order. We can only surmise that they may represent the defences of an earlier fort that was, as in other cases, superseded by a smaller one. The recorded finds consist of part of an amphora and an axe.[1] The present name is Gaelic, meaning 'strath of the marsh';[2] the Roman name, according to Mr Richmond, was Victoria.

Strageath would appear to be the parting of the ways. One might expect branch roads from it north-westwards to the fort of Dalginross and north to Fendoch. But there is no trace of any such roads, whose existence can only be presumed on *a priori* grounds. Before proceeding eastwards towards Perth we must make excursions to these two outlying forts.

The Roman site at Dalginross (Fig. 10) lies on the eastern edge of the Ruchil valley about half a mile south of the Earn at Comrie. The Ruchil valley is bounded on the east by a low cliff on the edge of which are the remains of two enclosures, one within the other. The inner one has two perfect sides 400 ft. long, the northern ends of the other two being cut off by the cliff. Some 200 ft. south-east of the south-east rampart is the only complete side of the outer enclosure, which is just over 500 ft. in length. These are the remains of two forts probably of different ages; there is no doubt that both are Roman. Between the two perfect (south-east) sides, the possible remains of another rampart, which seems to turn and continue westwards at each end, can be detected, though there is no evidence of such on the earlier plans. They do, however, show a marching-camp of which there are faint traces on the ground. I managed to get two sets of air-photos taken of the whole area, but both sets were taken at the wrong time of year and under the wrong lighting conditions, and they show little that was not already known from groundwork. The older plans vary and are inconsistent with each other. An old cadastral map of 1767, belonging to Mr Carmichael of Dalginross, shows the 'track of a casway', but owing to the great changes that have taken place here since then it is impossible to plot its exact course on the modern map. A plan[3] by George McFarlane of Comrie, dated 1802, is in the Perth Museum, together with a description by Mr McDiarmid, Minister of Comrie, which was presented to the Perth Society in 1807. An earlier and better plan, dated 1786, by 'a young gentleman residing in its neighbourhood', also now preserved at Perth, has

1 *P.S.A.S.* v (2), 1865, p. 241.
2 *Srath-gaoithe*; Watson, *Celtic Place-names*, p. 493.　　　3 Scale 1 : 264.

been reproduced by Sir George Macdonald.[1] It records a Roman road running south-westwards from the south-west gate of the outer fort to a 'pretty little mount called Castell Doin Dalig', which is still visible as a low mound in a ploughed field 360 ft. east of the farm of Newton. At the point

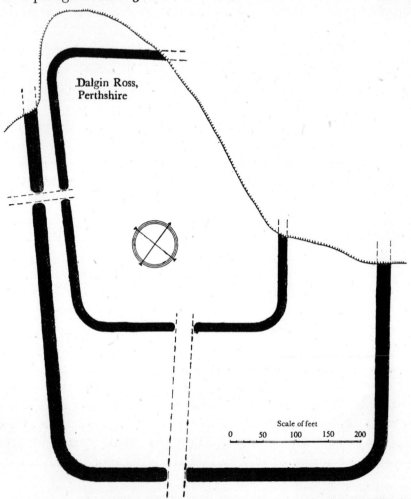

Fig. 10. Plan of two superimposed forts (from air-photographs), after Richmond.

where this road leaves the fort the young gentleman recorded the tradition of 'a kind of subterraneous passage' by which 'water was made to run eastward through the camp'. He dismisses it as 'a fable', recording, however, another 'small acqueduct from Rouchell water which came east somewhere about the New Manse, and entered the [marching-] camp at the south-west

1 *P.S.A.S.* LXXIII (1939), p. 253.

corner'. As Sir George says, these aqueducts (which I suspect to be one and the same—for a marching-camp would never have had one) may be less of a fable than the young gentleman supposed; 'the "tradition" may well be founded on the exposure of an underground channel'; and Sir George refers in support to the recent discoveries of aqueducts at Fendoch and Birrens.

There have been no excavations here, and until there have we must be content to know that there was certainly a Roman marching-camp and one, perhaps two, forts. The only finds consist of a gold coin of Vespasian (A.D. 70–9), found before 1786, and a coin of Domitian (A.D. 81–96) found within the area of the fort about 1905. A coin of Alexander Severus (A.D. 222–35) is said to have been picked up within or near the fort. The first two coins, together perhaps with the marching-camp, speak of occupation in the first century.

Pennant[1] refers to a 'multitude of oblong hollows that lie parallel, and divided from one another by banks three feet wide, which are to be seen just on the outside of the northern *Agger* of the camp'. He got the school-master to dig into them, with the result that large quantities of wood-charcoal were found. Were they ovens? It is not quite clear where they were, but of course the usual place for the ovens of a fort was *inside*, and sometimes actually in, the rampart. Were they *lilia*?

The causeway of the Roman road may still be seen issuing from the south gate of the fort; it can be traced for 800 ft. to the edge of the Ruchil escarpment where it appears to end. Another issues from the east gate and can be traced for about the same distance to the hedge where the hump of the causeway is distinctly visible. Beyond these there is not a trace of either road, unless a fragment of coarse road metal in the road leading to Cowden may indicate the course of one of them. This metal is in the direct line of the road. The first suggests a road to the missing fort at Callander; it can only have passed up Glen Artney, over a wild moorland region where some traces of it should survive. Such traces should be plainly seen from the air; and it was for the purpose of looking for them that we flew up Glen Artney in 1939. The visibility was perfect, but we could see nothing; and for once I feel confident in stating that there never was such a road. I feel almost as confident that the other road, which aims at a point between Ardoch and Strageath, was never made, for I have hunted everywhere for it in the only places where it can possibly have negotiated the very steep escarpment to the south-east. There are only two such points—above the Mill of Fortune and

1 *Tour*, 2nd ed. (1776), Part II, p. 98.

below Glentarf—and in neither of them (with the possible and very doubt-ful exception mentioned above) are any traces to be found.

The existence of short lengths of road is certain; is it possible that the making of such was carried out as part of the regular routine of fort-construction or that the construction of the main lengths of the road was postponed to a later date, and sometimes, as here, never carried out? From some other forts—Inchtuthil and Castle Carey for instance—there issue roads which seem to end prematurely, though of course this may eventually be found not to be so. But the hypothesis seems worth consideration. The making of branch roads to join outlying forts to the main road might well be the last item on a programme which here was never completed. The function of the Roman fort at Dalginross was no doubt to block the gate out of the Highlands by the Earn valley. It is significant that 4 miles higher up the Earn valley is the famous fort of Dundurn, mentioned as a tribal fort in the Dark Ages.

Dalginross has been identified by Mr Richmond with Ptolemy's Banatia.[1] The name means 'peaked' and is based on a word common to three Celtic languages meaning horn or peak.[2] No more suitable name could be imagined for a fort placed amid the peaks of the Highlands which overlook it on three sides and are still called Ben—Ben Clach on the south, Ben Halton and Mor Ben dominating it on the south-west, Ben Chonzie towering 3000 ft. above on the north. The name Dalginross means 'thorny point', and is eminently suitable to the site, which is still partly covered by furze. The name Comrie (Gaelic, *Cuimrigh*) means confluence; it stands at the junction of the Earn, Lednock and Ruchil rivers.

The fort of Dalginross blocked the route which led westwards through highland valleys to the sea. The wild intervening country must have been at most very thinly populated; but the coastlands of Argyll were not only themselves fertile and full of people but provided possible landing-places for outflanking Irish levies: hence the importance in later times of the castles of Dunolly, Dunadd and Dumbarton. These rocky outposts might guard the north-eastern plains as effectively as Stirling and Perth; but the Romans never got there,[3] and had to be content with blocking the other ends of the routes. The next block-house was at Fendoch, about 6 miles north-east of Crieff, at the mouth of Glenalmond. And here a word of explanation is necessary. The name 'Glenalmond' has come to be used for that part of

1 *P.S.A.S.* LVI (1922), p. 296.    2 Watson, *Celtic Place-names*, p. 31.
3 Except for a time, to Dumbarton; see Macdonald, *Roman Wall*, 2nd ed. pp. 186–8.

the Almond valley which lies between the southern debouchment of the Sma'
Glen and Trinity College; but properly this part should be called Logie-
almond, that part of Almond which lies in the hollow.[1] This is quite clear
from the descriptions of earlier writers, one of whom specifically states that
'the country is not called Glenalmond to the eastward' of Buchanty.[2]

Glenalmond was the name of the valley from its head south of Loch Tay
to the mouth of the Sma' Glen at Fendoch; and the Sma' Glen was merely
the narrow south-eastern end, and was formerly so called. The Narrow Glen
is strategically important, not because it leads up Glenalmond but because
it also leads by an easy pass northwards to Strath Bran at Amulree. This
fact was observed both by Agricola and his successor, General Wade, who
used the Narrow Glen for his road to Inverness. For Agricola the route was
important because it completely outflanked his headquarters at Inchtuthil
and the whole defence system organized round it.

The remains at Fendoch consist of an Agricolan fort, rediscovered and
excavated in 1936 and 1937 by Messrs Ian Richmond and James McIntyre;
a fragmentary earthwork on the north-west called 'redoubt' on the Ordnance map; and an alleged marching-camp. Besides these there were cairns,
graves, hut-circles and other remains of unknown age on the east, and a
round stone tower on Tom-nam-brach, a hill to the north-west.

The Roman fort was discovered, it seems, by Colonel Shand, whose first
reference to it is dated 1788.[3] There is, however, an earlier reference to it
in 1784 and others in certain manuscript accounts written about this time
and preserved in the Perth Library. These do not necessarily invalidate
Colonel Shand's claim to be the discoverer; what does appear to, however,
is his statement, in 1801,[4] that the *camp* at Fendoch 'contains, as usual, about
90 acres Scots measure, and is advantageously situated in the mouth of
Glen Amon'. This area is equivalent to 113·5 English acres. The area of the
camp (not the fort) is given on the 1778 plan (Plate VI) as 57 acres 3 roods
37 furlongs. In any case the areas are all too large for the *fort*. But Colonel
Shand could never have missed seeing the fort if he was there at all—as we
know he was; so the point ceases to have much interest.

The fort covers about 44 acres and is rectangular, 598 × 320 ft. surrounded
by a turf rampart and ditch (see plan opposite p. 46). Each side had an entrance

---

1 From *logaigh*, dative of *logach*, 'place in the hollow'; Watson, *Celtic Place-names*, p. 147.
2 Antiquarian Notes on Glenalmond, *c.* 1783; MS. No. 126 in Perth Library.
3 *P.S.A.S.* LXXI, 374.
4 In a letter to Chalmers, quoted in *Caledonia*, I, 146, note f.

gate, strongly defended with wooden towers (Fig. 11). Inside, the buildings were all of wood, the timber being imported, for pollen analysis has shown that none was available in the district. At the west end stood the four barrack-rows, separated by the Via Principalis from the rest of the fort. In the middle was the headquarters building, flanked on the north by granaries and on the south by the Commandant's house, a 'neat residential structure', as the auctioneer would call it, with a central court surrounded by rooms—a dining-room, bedrooms, bathroom and the 'usual offices'. Behind it was the hospital, and the east end again held barracks. Immediately under the

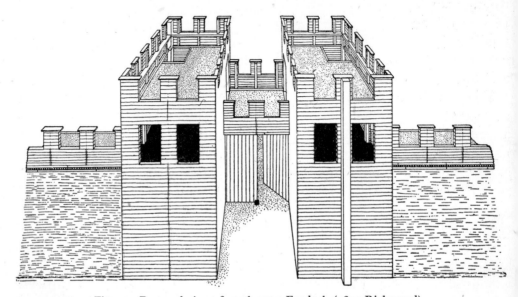

Fig. 11. Restored view of north gate, Fendoch (after Richmond).

rampart were ovens and perhaps piles of stores; and between them and the buildings a metalled road ran round the fort.

Of all these timber buildings only the post-holes and sleeper-trenches remained. It is suggested that the timber fittings were standardized and made to a regulation pattern by legionary carpenters at the base head-quarters. Certain it is that they were dismantled and removed, for even the damage to the sides of the sleeper-trenches done by the demolition gangs was detected by the superb technique of the excavators. No doubt it was intended to re-use the timber elsewhere. Some of the excavator's finest work was devoted to the excavation and reconstruction, on paper, of the gateways. Plate VII shows two of the post-holes for the timbers of the south gateway, with Mr Richmond explaining the position to Sir George Macdonald (taken 24 June 1937). Fig. 11 gives a reconstructed elevation of the north gate; it will be noticed that the timber framework is covered by weather-boards. It might be thought that this is pure conjecture; but that is not so. The weather-boarding is not purely conjectural; it was *inferred* from the fact that, where the fallen turf of the rampart abutted against the sides of the wooden gate-towers, it was found to end abruptly, several courses remaining standing and still visible. 'Thus the rampart had evidently been laid up against the boarding.'[1] Where such meticulous observations, and the inferences thereby provided, were not possible, the reconstruction is based upon the illustrations on Trajan's column and on the analogy of similar sites excavated on the German frontier and elsewhere. I stress these facts because the achievements of modern excavating technique are still little known; they have advanced far ahead of the possibilities of using them in a country which is still dominated by a bookish and clerical conception of culture.

The 'redoubt' is a puzzling earthwork, whose affairs are mixed up with those of the alleged marching-camp. Both first appear in a plan (preserved in the Perth Library) drawn in 1778 by J. McOmie, where the 'redoubt' is marked as an excrescence on the larger camp. As may be seen (Plate VI), this plan does not mark the fort at all. The existing remains of the redoubt consist of a bank 70 yards long with a ditch on the north and two rounded corners, and the remains of two other sides, 23 yards long on the west and 20 yards on the east. In the middle of the north side the bank is broken, more or less, by a gap 10 yards wide, from the east end of which runs a stony bank, 8 yards long, towards the interior. Between this earthwork and the modern road, parallel to the latter, is a marshy gully (possibly the 'Smith's well' of an eighteenth-century description). The western bank is about 5 ft. above the bottom of the ditch. There is a pit near the south end of the west bank, inside the area. I first inspected these remains in 1925, and noted that they were 'possibly Roman'; and I saw no reason to alter my opinion when I revisited the site in 1940. But attached 'redoubts' have no place in the design of a Roman marching-camp, even supposing the one here to be authenticated. Its true character must await further investigations.

The alleged marching-camp as marked on the plan encloses the greater part of the area between the Almond on the north and the Fendoch burn on the south. The sides are laid out in straight sections, but no gaps or entrances

1 *P.S.A.S.* LXXIII, 117.

are shown. I have not been able to inspect the site and test it since I did not discover the plan at Perth until too late to do so. Here I would take the opportunity of expressing my most grateful thanks to Mr Thomas McLaren, formerly Burgh Surveyor of Perth, and to Mr McLaren and Mr Wood, as well as to the late Mr Ritchie, all of Perth Library, and to Dr Malcolm of the Signet Library, for their generous help. The documents and plans which they have unearthed and placed at my disposal have been of the greatest assistance. Mr Thomas McLaren has also helped by his great knowledge of the Perth district.

This already none too straightforward site was still further complicated by Dr Christison, who saw the earthworks and published a plan of parts of them.[1] Unfortunately, misled it seems by local information, he mistook some obviously modern enclosure-banks for the western corner of the marching-camp; and it is these that are marked on his plan. By a curious and rather tiresome coincidence the plan of these banks, even down to an attached 'redoubt', closely duplicates that of the marching-camp with its 'redoubt' as marked on the plan of 1778. But there is no doubt at all that, whatever their respective ages, the two 'redoubts' were distinct, for they are still there; the western one—Dr Christison's—has nearly the same dimensions as the other, but the bank and ditch are much smaller and not of a defensive nature.

The north-west corner of this alleged camp rested on a hill called Tom-nam-brach where the account of c. 1783 records the presence of an old 'castle' about 60 yards in circumference. Many of the stones were removed in 1783 to build the adjacent bridge just below, over the Almond. The name should probably be read 'Tom-nam-broch', the hillock of the broch or fort.

To the east was once a group of cairns, some of which are marked on the plan of 1778. They were first recorded by John Gillies, the bookseller of Perth, who published a description of his 'One day's journey to the Highlands of Scotland, March 12th 1784'. He saw 'a great number of cairns or graves of the Caledonians or Danes, some of which are placed regularly in rows', and also 'burying-places of the Romans, or small *tumuli*, covered with turf'. His desire to open them was frustrated by lack of time; he covered 40 miles in his day's outing, and any excavations he might have made would not be likely to have done much good. The writer of 1783 also refers to these remains. Never easy to follow, his account here excels itself. After referring to certain round and crescent-shaped objects, probably hut-circles, he continues: 'There is one in particular within which is four or five stones set up,

1 *Early Fortifications* (1898), p. 92, fig. 29.

with one in the middle larger than the rest, something resembling hair; it is said to be a place where courts were held for the trial of criminals, as there is a hillock beside it called Tom-na-croich or the Gallows hill, where formerly people was executed. There was one Stewart hanged here who was condemned at the regality court of Loggierate.' The stone resembling hair may have been a standing-stone whose apex had been worn into irregular grooves by the prolonged action of rain-water; but this is merely a guess.

No Roman roads have been found at Fendoch. But the plan of 1778 now shows that the 'lightly-metalled disused road' not more than 12 ft. wide which the excavators found south of the fort[1] and recognized as modern, was the old road from Glenalmond to Perth. The hollow tracks of this road, or its medieval forerunner, are still plainly visible in the triangular area between the modern roads immediately north of the cross-roads west of the fort. At Wester Fendoch (now gone) there came in from the west another old but non-Roman road which may be traced, with breaks, south of Fendoch and Connachan farms, to Monzie, where it crossed the Shaggie Burn by an old single-arched bridge still in existence, but disused, immediately above the present bridge. North of Monzie this road can be traced through the middle of an oval native fort on Knock Durroch; just as near Fendoch, the road is bounded by larger stones set as a curb and is about 12 ft. wide. Everywhere it has gone completely out of use. It is distinct from General Wade's road, whose course can here be followed quite easily. It must, therefore, be its predecessor for part of its course. Though once thought to be Roman, it is quite definitely non-Roman in character.

What may have been a linear earthwork east of the Roman fort is thus described in the unpublished 'Antiquarian Notes on Glenalmond' (c. 1783: Perth Library, No. 126, pp. 16, 17 of the typescript): 'About 300 yards distant from the great trench of the camp is a straight line drawn across this plain from the river Almond on the north to the hill on the south, cutting off the greatest part of the plain to the eastward; and there is other lines at the same distance from the first. These seem to be outlines belonging to the camp.' They may, however, have been merely old enclosure-banks. The only printed record of an alleged Roman road to Fendoch is contained in a letter which Chalmers tells us[2] he received from 'the late inquisitive Colonel Shand, who had inspected that vicinity [Fendoch] with the eye of a soldier'. The letter was dated 22 December 1801. Shand there stated that the road was 12 ft. wide, very distinct in places, and that he had traced it 'from the confluence

1 *P.S.A.S.* LXXIII, 115.          2 *Caledonia*, I, 146.

of the Powaffray water with the river Ern, near Strageth...through the country northward to the plantations of Monzie, where there is the vestige of a strong post in the Roman style; from which post this vicinal way turns to the right; and I was told by some of the country people that it may still be seen, in a few places, running on past Connachan to the Roman camp at East Findoch'. Shand was as a rule sound on Roman forts and camps; but, as here, he was apt to mistake native forts for Roman outposts—they are not always easy to distinguish even to-day; and he suffered from delusions about 'vicinal ways'. From the above-quoted description, I have no doubt that he was referring to the road described above, which I know well and have followed on foot or bicycle for many miles. South of Gilmerton it runs pretty straight to Dalpatrick, where there is a ford across the Earn, and thence on to Auchterarder. We may regard it as an important medieval road that was metalled in the seventeenth or eighteenth century. There is nothing Roman about it either in alignment or construction. No one would claim the culverts beneath it at Fendoch or the bridge at Monzie as Roman; nor did the Romans waste their time metalling the native trackways of Scotland, as Dr Christison believed.

We have now disposed of the two branch-forts, and shall be able in the next chapter to resume our course at Strageath. There is between that fort and Perth a line of signal-posts of great interest; and near Perth itself are the chief Roman remains in our area.

# Chapter Four

## STRAGEATH TO COUPAR ANGUS

WE left the main road at the fort of Strageath on the Earn. The disposition of the roads leading out of Strageath is curious and lends some support to the theory that they were made before the main road was laid out, and that the main road itself had to adapt its course to them. In spite of long-continued cultivation they can be traced, by a combination of ground and air observation, with considerable certainty. The main road picks up the road issuing from the north gate of Strageath at a point 720 ft. north of the gate, and continues in a north-easterly direction, aiming at Coblehaugh, the point where the Earn turns south-eastwards, which, as the name indicates, was the site of the ferry. The exact Roman crossing-point is uncertain. Roy, followed by the Ordnance Survey, is probably wrong in putting it at the disused Creel ford, which has been obliterated by the canalization of the Pow Water.[1] A more likely place for the Roman bridge is at Innerpeffray ferry; there is still a ford here, where I crossed on foot, with my bicycle, on 25 June 1925.

For a mile the road is lost, but there is no doubt that its course as marked on the Ordnance map is correct. It is first visible in a wood at Parkneuk where there is also the first of a series of nine circular signal-posts along the road. These now consist of a roundish platform, usually about 40 ft. across, surrounded by a ditch with a gap for the entrance causeway on the side next to the road. Within was a broad turf-bank protecting the base of a high wooden tower 12 ft. square, supported by four massive timber up-rights. These towers have been compared with their stone equivalents, the mile-castles on Hadrian's Wall. Similar towers are depicted on Trajan's column[2] where a torch projecting from the upper story shows that they were designed for signalling.[3] One such signal-post has been mentioned

[1] In the fork between the Pow Water and Earn here in 1939 I observed the outline of a native fort, as I thought, in a cornfield; but it is possible that I was misled by an old meander of the river.

[2] Plate LX, 1, fig. 1, of Macdonald's *Roman Wall*, 2nd ed. 1934.

[3] Sir Robert Sibbald (*Portus, coloniae et castella Romana* [1711], p. 5) refers to the 'nitidae speculae' of Statius (A.D. 45–96) which he regarded as 'high towers' placed along the coast

between Camelon and Stirling; I discovered at least one from the air near the Beef-tub; there is one near Bewcastle, another near Reycross and several others elsewhere, though none has been found in the south of England. Another, at Meikleour, has been excavated and described by Mr Richmond[1] (Fig. 18). Except for the last, all these posts are known to be on roads; their purpose was doubtless to send code messages to military headquarters, primarily in cases of hostile attack. It stands to reason that a signal-post, unless it were the link between two forts—and no such instance is known—implies others; and an exciting field of research is opened up for, within limits, it is possible to forecast approximately the position of these posts. They must be mutually intervisible and therefore on high ground. They will not be far from the road they serve; and they will not be much more than a mile apart. The distances which separate these posts on the Gask ridge range from 2660 ft. to 1 mile 1500 ft. and average 4382 ft. (0·83 of a mile, about four-fifths), and it is probable that these nine form a complete series extending for a stretch of 6½ miles. Six of them were excavated (one only 'partially') by the Society of Antiquaries in 1900, under the direction of Dr Christison; but plans of only two of these were published and the descriptions of the remaining four were confined to a few lines. No relics whatever were found and their exact date within the Roman period remains therefore unproven.

I have numbered the signal-posts afresh, starting from the west. No. 1 in Parkneuk wood has already been mentioned. No. 2 (Raith) was found in March 1901[2] 'in the course of sinking a pit for holding a water-tank on the farm of Raith', at a spot marked on the 6 in. map by a triangle and the spot-level 299 ft. No. 3 (Ardunie) was found by me quite accidentally as I was walking along the Roman road on 1 June 1937. It is on the south side of the

and described as 'nitidae' by the poet 'because of the lights, shining in the night, which were placed upon them'. The relevant passage is as follows:

> Hic suetus dare jura parens, hoc cespite turmas
> Affari nitidas speculas castellaque longe
> Aspicis; ille dedit cinxitque haec moenia fossa,
> Belligeris haec dona deis, haec tela dicavit.
> Cernis adhuc titulos: hunc ipse vacantibus armis
> Induit, hunc regi rapuit thoraca Britanno.

1 *P.S.A.S.* LXXIV (1940), pp. 37–40.
2 That is, about three months *after* the account of the excavations was read before the Society (on 30 November 1900). No doubt the facts were added between reading and setting the article in type: see the Report, *P.S.A.S.* XXXV (1901), p. 28.

road, immediately adjacent to it. The diameter of the platform is 13 yards. The site is marked by a large beech-tree growing on the south road-bank. No. 4 (Kirkhill) is also on the south side and in a wood; it was excavated in 1900. The ditch has a bank round it on the outside. When I visited it in 1937 to plot it on the map it was honeycombed with rabbit-burrows. No. 5 (Muir o' Fauld) is also on the south side and is the one that was only partially excavated. Signs of these activities are still evident in the centre of the mound, which is 35 yards south of the centre of the road. The diameter of the mound is 52 ft. The ditch is 11 ft. wide on the west side; a causeway 8 ft. 6 in. wide and 9 ft. long leads across it towards the road. The ditch had been full of water shortly before my visit (4 July 1925) but was then dry. No. 6 (Gask) is marked on the Ordnance map (Perthshire, Sheet 108 N.E.) and is the last to be placed on the south side of the road. It was excavated in 1900.

Immediately to the south of it was a rectangular Roman fort of the semi-permanent kind. The only record of this is in an anonymous manuscript of 1789 belonging to the Society of Antiquaries of Scotland where a plan of it[1] is given. This records gateways protected by straight traverses on the east and west sides a little to the north of their middle points, and a similar gateway in the middle of the north side. Part of the west portion of the south side, including entrance and traverse (if any), is marked as missing. Christison records the sides as measuring about 470 × 400 ft.[2] The rampart consisted of a single bank and ditch. He was unable to find any superficial traces of this fort, but claims to have recovered the whole by the 'numerous cuts' he made, including even the missing traverse in the south side. The ditch thus found was, however, only 3 ft. wide and 18 *inches* deep; and he concluded that these were 'suggestive of the first marking out, or beginning, of a camp, rather than of a finished work'.[3] It will be agreed that a fort defended by a ditch 18 in. deep with a rampart of corresponding height would not have presented a very formidable obstacle to attack. Christison admits experiencing 'some difficulty in identifying the camp trench, as many drainage-ditches crossed the space', and it seems probable that the supposed 'camp trench' was in reality a synthetic product compounded of these and of wishful thoughts. Christison himself seems to have had misgivings, for he published no plan or measurements, so that it is not even possible to locate

---

1 Reproduced by Christison in *P.S.A.S.* xxxv, 35.
2 I make the internal area, as measured on the old plan, about 450 × 370 ft., and the area with the defences included about 550 × 450 ft.
3 *P.S.A.S.* xxxv, 36.

the site to-day, except approximately from the old plan; and his account of the whole excavation occupies only thirteen lines.

I visited the site in June 1937 to try and discover the outline of the fort, but failed to do so. Part of the presumed area was occupied by a decayed plantation, encumbered with fallen trees and a matted growth of rank weeds. Even to walk over it was difficult, and to detect the remains of old banks and ditches quite impossible, for one could not even see the ground. I saw some banks and ditches but they were small and obviously quite modern. The southern part of the presumed area was under grass but had been for long under cultivation and nothing could be seen. If this part is now again cultivated the crops should reveal the outline of the old fort on an air-photograph. The site is about 1700 ft. north-east of Gask House.

No. 7 lies on the north side of the road, 100 yards from it. It is called Witch Knowe on the Ordnance map, which records the discovery here of human skeletons in 1855. It was 'very completely' excavated by Dr Christison, who published a plan showing four post-holes, about 18 in. in diameter and 2 ft. deep, defining a rectangular space 11 × 9 ft., measured from the centre of the post-holes. The interior platform was 44 ft. across, surrounded by a ditch 14 ft. wide and 6 ft. deep enclosed by a bank 18 ft. wide. The entrance causeway was 6 ft. wide.

No. 8 (Moss-side) lies on the north side of the road, 70 yards from it. It was excavated by Christison whose plan and description show that the base of the wooden tower was surrounded by a turf bank about 14 ft. wide and 3 ft. high, comparing well with that at Black Hill, Meikleour, which was 12 ft. wide and 3 ft. 8 in. high. (Christison did not recognize the turf structure of the bank, but this feature can safely be inferred from his description of it as 'composed of about ten alternate layers of black mould and yellow or red clay'.) The post-holes were 11 ft. apart and 'connected by flat cuts, probably to hold beams', clearly sleeper-trenches. In 1900 the field was under plough, but the inner area was still unploughed. It is now ploughed all over, and when I visited it in 1925 the ditch showed up very plainly as a circle of darker corn. In 1940 the ditch was hardly visible; but the central area was conspicuous as a dark disk in a field of a light reddish colour.

No. 9, the last, is on the north side of the road on a natural hillock of igneous rock about 500 × 200 ft., called in 1789 Thorny Hill or the Hill of Midgeat (not Midgeal as Christison misread it). On the east end of it Christison claims to have found a small fort and he may be right, though I saw nothing but a ditch running across the hill from north to south, possibly the western defence of the fort. On the west end was found the circular ditch of a signal-post enclosing an area 50 × 35 ft., with a break in the south side. No post-holes were found, but in the middle was an oblong area 7 × 4 ft., with some stones enclosed by a setting of curb-stones. Two similar areas were found in the adjacent fort. When I first visited the site in 1925 I failed to find the signal-post because I assumed that it would be where it is marked on the Ordnance map.[1] But there was nothing on the ground, so far as I could see, to represent the round bank there marked, and in 1940 I found the signal-post on the west end of the hill about 200 ft. west of the Ordnance site.

The Roman road beside which these signal-posts are placed is used as a grassy track from the Crieff-Auchterarder road for just over 2 miles to a point where the road from Gask Church comes into it from the south. From here eastwards it is a modern metalled road. But I would warn intending explorers that the grassy track is in places so much overgrown that it is difficult to force one's way along it. I managed to do so in June 1937, and even to push or carry my bicycle through, and I was rewarded by the discovery of signal-post No. 3, which I might well have missed if my progress had been more smooth and rapid. I also noted a well-preserved part of the Roman causeway a little to the west of it between the two Ardunies. Further east there is a stretch of about 1000 ft. of causeway visible on the north side of the modern road, between the wood on the west and the east boundary of the field in which signal-post No. 8 stands. That is the last point where it is visible and we shall not, unfortunately, rejoin it until we have crossed the Tay at Scone, and then only for a moment. A quarter of a mile north-east of signal-post No. 9 the modern road bends northwards; I thought I could see the track of the Roman road continuing in the same alignment eastwards, in the form of a stony belt across a ploughed field; but this ended on the east side of the field and I could find no trace of it beyond. How it reached 'Bertha' is a problem that has hitherto defied solution, though I have twice flown over the intervening area to look for it, and Mr Bradley, while acting as Flying Instructor in the neighbourhood in 1940, also hunted for it in vain. Mr Thomas McLaren, late Burgh Surveyor of Perth, has also failed to find any traces of it during his long experience of archaeological work in the district. Nor do the older writers help. The northern slopes of the Drum of Gask have been cultivated more intensively than the rest of the area. In September 1943 Dr St Joseph, from the air, saw the crop-mark of the road continuing a mile further eastwards, beyond the last signal-station, and

1 Perthshire, 97 s.w.

thought he could see another signal-post. His account has not yet appeared in print.

There is one possible clue, though it may be a false one. Pennant,[1] who passed by there in 1772,[2] says that at Tibbermore, which is near the middle of this missing stretch, 'below the minister's house is a rhomboid entrenchment called "the Ward"'. A rhomboid entrenchment suggests a Roman fort or camp whose lay-out was not mathematically exact—and there are several such camps. Accordingly I visited Tibbermore in 1940, and I did find a short length (about 260 ft.) of bank running south-westwards from the road from a point just north of the church path. It is broad and stony with trees growing on it, and is evidently older than the present field-system with whose alignment it is unconformable. Moreover, it does combine with other features to make a rhomboid figure with sides approximately 600 ft. long, and its position agrees with Pennant's description. But there is no concrete evidence beyond the bank referred to, and even this is ambiguous; nor is there any evidence at all of age. One would like to connect it with the missing portion of the Roman road, and the north-west and south-east sides are (if my hypothesis has any foundation in fact) parallel to its presumed alignment. If that alignment is correct the Roman road should pass by the famous medieval castle of Huntingtower, as Roy suggested. Mr Bradley spent much time looking for the road here and at Tibbermore, but he saw nothing that can be regarded as certain, nor do his photographs reveal anything of relevance. (In passing I must record that the 'high copped tumulus or mount, styled the Round Law' mentioned by Pennant hereabouts is probably to be identified with a high and well-preserved mound in the road-fork between the large disused quarry on the east and Almondbank station at Lochty on the north-north-west. It is not marked on the map.)

And now we reach the Tay with its important group of Roman sites (Fig. 12). These consist of the permanent fort of 'Bertha'—the name is a ghost-word but convenient—the marching-camp of Grassy Wells and the temporary fort of Gold Castle (both in Scone Park), and the outlying fort at Carpow on the south bank of the Tay estuary below Abernethy. Originally no doubt the administrative centre must have been at Inchtuthil, but for convenience we must sacrifice logic and deal with it and the sites round it separately. The framework of this account is topographical rather than

1 Ed. Pinkerton, III (1809), p. 411.
2 Elsewhere (2nd ed. [1776], II, 89) he definitely states that the Roman road went 'by Tibbermore and Bertha'; but he does not describe it, and I do not think he saw it.

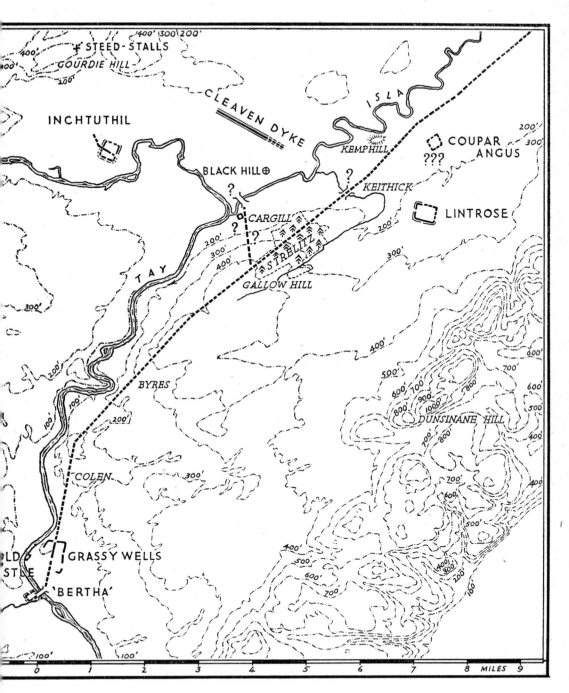

Fig. 12. 'Bertha' to Coupar Angus.

historical. The key-site is the fort of 'Bertha', but before tackling it we must secure our flank and rear, approaching our main objective indirectly, in accordance with the soundest military strategy.

Carpow can quickly be disposed of. It stands on a bluff $1\frac{1}{2}$ miles north-east of Abernethy, overlooking the estuary of the Tay near the mouth of the Earn, and it is certainly the site of a coastal fort, but when I wrote the first draft of this book only the baths had been found, and no remains of the fort itself had come to light. Since then, Dr St Joseph, flying over the site in September 1943, has seen remains of the ramparts and subsequently identified them on the ground. Most of the outline of the fort is visible as a crop-mark, with two ditches round the south and east sides. 'It is also', he adds, 'visible on the ground, when you know where to look. The area within the rampart-centre works out at about some twelve and a half acres, though, to be quite safe, one should say this might include an annexe' (letter of 19 Sept. 1943). Two Roman coins have been found, one of Faustina, suggesting, so far as its slender evidence goes, a second-century date.[1] Carpow was long ago identified with Ptolemy's Horrea by Mr Richmond[2] and later with the Poreoclassis (Horrea Classis?) of the Ravenna geographer. It was the obvious supply-base for a campaign in Strathmore. Geographically Carpow belongs to the peninsula lying between the Forth and Tay estuaries; and in the whole of this area, bounded on the west and north by Strathearn and Strathallan, and comprising the counties of Fife, Kinross and Clackmannan, there have been found, apart from Carpow, no Roman forts or other military sites and hardly any objects of Roman character except a few coins. That air-photography will reveal some may be regarded as almost certain. The only site in the region of which I have seen an air-photograph is Lochore, which has been claimed as a Roman fort;[3] but both from this photograph and from inspection on the ground I think a medieval date more probable. There are of course a host of claimants, but most of the candidates can be disposed of without ceremony. The most promising one is an unlocated rectangular earthwork near Auchterderran which has yielded a coin of Pertinax (A.D. 192–3).[4]

Colonel Shand thought he could trace a Roman road running from Carpow towards Dunning and Duncrub. It was to be seen 'almost perfect

1 Sir George Macdonald, *P.S.A.S.* LII, 232.
2 *P.S.A.S.* LVI, 289. 3 Gordon, *Itin. Sept.* 36, and see pp. 144–6 below.
4 *P.S.A.S.* LII, 238. I looked in vain for it on the most likely ground in October 1943. See p. 146 below.

for more than a mile through the moorish ground called Muirmonth', where it was 16 ft. wide, raised above the adjacent ground, with a ditch on each side.[1] It was called a 'vicinal way', which generally means that the road so called is not Roman. It would be worth investigation, but, although some such road seems required to connect Carpow with the interior, I do not feel quite happy about this one, as described, nor do I feel convinced that any such road was ever made.

The region traversed is rich in remains of other periods; but the only site ever claimed as Roman is the so-called 'Roman camp' at Ardargie, 2¾ miles south-east of Forteviot. Here is a moat 38 ft. wide, situated on the steep slopes of the east side of the May valley, enclosing a square platform 200 ft. across. There was originally a bank on *both* sides of the moat, the outer bank being now preserved best on the lower (south-west) side. The east side rests on a steep gully, but there are faint possible traces of the inner bank, and the ditch is absent. There is no entrance-gap. The site and visible remains have nothing Roman about them and a medieval or Dark Age date is more likely.

At the other end, half a mile north-north-east of Dunning Church, in Kincladie wood, is preserved a short length (430 ft.) of bank and ditch. It crosses the south end of the wood, leaving the Dunning-Forteviot road obliquely, on the west side of it. The top of the bank is about 3 or 4 ft. above the bottom of the ditch which is on the north side. I came across this earthwork quite by chance; but it is doubtless the 'trench' referred to by Macfarlane[2] 'in a level muir' north-east of Dunning, on the way to Perth. When I rediscovered it I took it to be a linear earthwork or cross-dyke barrier over the north-east approaches to Dunning. But the possibility that it might be a fragment of a Roman camp, which did not occur to me on the spot, cannot be altogether excluded.

Having thus cleared the ground in our rear we can safely approach 'Bertha' (Plate VIII). The fort stands at the mouth of the river Almond, on a spur of land between that river and the Tay, 2½ miles north-west of Perth. The north and south sides measure 840 and 879 ft., and the east and west sides 450 and 564 ft. respectively, according to the late Mr Callander, whose very full description of the site, which he investigated in 1917 with Mr Thomas McLaren, then Burgh Surveyor of Perth, makes a lengthy account unnecessary here.[3] Callander and McLaren have shown that, for once, Roy's plan is incorrect. He saw the south-east side of the fort, on the brow of the

1 Chalmers, *Caledonia*, I, 146.          2 *Geogr. Collections*, I, 121.
3 *P.S.A.S.* LIII (1919), pp. 145-52.

Almond cliff, but mistook it for the north-west side of a fort that had been destroyed by the river. Actually the south-west and north-west sides can still be seen in the ploughed field through which the railway runs. There is a gap in the middle of the north-west side; the mound of the rampart is sometimes visible against the lighter background by a combination of sunlight and shadow which I was fortunate enough to catch with my camera. Having walked and flown over the site many times I can confirm the accuracy of the published description.

No coins have been found in the fort, and the other finds made in the eighteenth century, though curious and interesting, are now lost and therefore unserviceable. They include a pig of lead and some pots, found just outside the fort on the west, at the bottom of shafts, 18 ft. deep, revealed in the side of the cliff.

The name 'Bertha' is fictitious and was invented in the fourteenth century by John of Fordoun; it does not occur in any ancient documents. In the Dark Ages it was called Rath-inver-amon, 'the fort at the mouth of the Amon'; and a hill between it and Perth, Tula Amain, is still called the Tulloch. Tulach (=Tulloch) means a hill. Tula Amain (genitive) is mentioned in the *Annals of Ulster* under the year 686. Here at the beginning of the eighteenth century Alexander Christie set up the first bleaching-ground, and was the first person who introduced the right culture of potatoes into Scotland. The name Inveralmond still survives as the name of an old house near Almond bridge. The name is derived from an Old Celtic word *Ambona*, a strengthened form of the word *Ambis*, a river, whose base *ab* has also produced *Abona*, the early form of the common river-name Avon.[1] Richmond has identified the fort at 'Bertha' with Ptolemy's place Tamia, and I find it difficult to dissociate this from the Tay, though the early forms disallow this. Watson has shown, however, that the early Gaelic name of the river Tay (*Tōe*) presupposes a form *Tavia*, and he would therefore emend Ptolemy's name for the river (*Tava*) accordingly. In early manuscripts the letters *m*, *n*, *u* and *i* are seldom distinguishable and Tamia differs only by one minim from Tauia.

The Tay is the broadest river in Scotland and was bridged here by the Romans, and if ever a fort invited such nomenclature it is 'Bertha'. Remains of the foundations of a wooden bridge were still visible here in 1795: 'it consists of large oak planks, from six to eight inches in diameter, fastened together by long skairs, but coarsely jointed, and surrounded with clasps of iron, frequently twisted...I caused one of them to be raised some years ago'.[2]

1 Watson, *Celtic Place-names*, p. 430.  2 *O.S.A.* xv, 528.

The site of this bridge is marked on the Ordnance map[1] doubtless copying Roy's plan, where six piers are shown over the river. The correct site, however, is almost certainly 100 yards higher up the river where a stony ridge crosses the river at right angles to its course, causing rapids plainly visible from the bank. From the air a distinct causeway of small boulders can be seen. Mr Bradley saw it often from the air and it can be seen quite plainly on one of his photographs. Below the bridge the Ordnance map marks the site of the disused so-called Derder's ford; and it is plain, from the slightly curved course, that here at any rate Roy's plan has been exactly copied. The stony ridge is plainly visible on the air-photograph (Plate VIII), but I am doubtful about 'Derder's ford'. The diagonal course is much more suggestive of a weir, such as those still existing across the river above and below Stanley, and on many other rivers in Scotland, England and elsewhere. But of course it might also have served as a ford. Mr Bradley did actually cross the river by means of it in 1940; and in 1941 he reported that the ridge of stones was clearly visible above water during a drought. His attempt to return by means of the other ridge (where the bridge is considered to have been) was frustrated by his meeting with 'sudden deeps'.

Of the road on the west side there is only a doubtful trace, plainly seen on an air-photograph as a dark band diagonally crossing a light-coloured field. Southwards it appears to reach the Almond at the point where the road-bridge was before the present bridge was built in 1827 (Fig. 13). But the dark band is not the former course of the modern road, for that also is visible, following a course which agrees roughly with that shown on Roy's plan. I am, however, suspicious of this dark band, for it should, according to the rules, indicate a ditch, not a causeway. There was nothing to be seen on the ground last May, but I could not examine the field thoroughly on account of growing crops. If this *is* a Roman road it must have gone to Inchtuthil—there is no other trace of such a road, and it may never have existed.

Two miles to the west is an earthwork on the north brow of the Almond bank at Pitcairnfield. A careful plan of it was made many years ago by Mr T. McLaren. It contains a small rectangular enclosure, which on the strength of it has been claimed as a signal-post; but this claim is of very doubtful authenticity. It will now become more difficult to establish since during the war the military authorities, with characteristic good taste, converted the interior into a latrine.

1 Perthshire, 85 S.E.

I have delayed rather long over 'Bertha' and we must hurry on over the Tay, where there are several very interesting sites. Before leaving, however, we must shed a passing tear in memory of the great battle of Luncarty, which has been described at length by earlier chroniclers. Alas, the Danes never fled in disorder over Turnagain hillock, nor did Hay the peasant rally the Scottish levies; no Danish king was buried at the King's Stone in Danemark Field, nor did the vanished burial-mounds beside it cover slaughtered warriors; they were, in all probability, the begetters of the story rather than the result of the battle, for the whole thing was invented by Hector Boece (1465?–1536), one of the three great falsifiers of Scottish history.[1]

Crossing the Tay at 'Bertha' we enter Scone Park at Legger Ley, and walking upstream along the east bank of the Tay we first pass the 'handsome square, inclosed with a rampart and ditch', mentioned by Maitland.[2] It is nearly opposite Broxy Kennels and is not now square, being 48 × 38 yards, but the west side may have been eroded by the river. Then, just beyond a clump of trees on a great bend of the river we come to Gold Castle, a Roman fort of the semi-permanent kind which has been overlooked for nearly 100 years.[3] The site is marked on the Ordnance map,[4] where a small square of broken lines is shown. The sides of the square, however, are less than 100 ft. in length and there is now nothing visible on the ground to correspond. I had never been able to visit the spot, but when flying to Aberdeen on the 7 June 1939, I saw out of the corner of my eye something that looked rectangular, and on the return journey I made a point of investigating it more

---

1 There seems also to have been a square earthwork at Luncarty, for on the unpublished 1755 map of Scotland in the British Museum (King's Library, XLVIII, p. 25, Sheet 17) a square 'Danish intrenchment' is marked at 'Longcartie' on the right bank of the Tay, between Shachy and Ordy bridges on the north and Fordsmill and Blackhall on the south. Since this must have been in Redgorton parish it can hardly be equated with the 'praetorium of a Roman camp' mentioned by the writer of the account of Monedie in the *O.S.A.* (III [1792], p. 274): no clue is given to its exact position on the map of Monedie parish and there is nothing to suggest it. The square earthwork may perhaps be the same as the 'long oval rampart of earth' on the land side of the King's Stone (see *The Muses' Threnodie* [1638], ed. by James Cant, Perth [1774], p. 50). The same editor also records the discovery, near some cott-houses called Danemark, about the year 1770, of 'the handle and part of the blade of a sword, which was sent to the Earl of Kinnoul'. A possible native fort or signal-post is indicated by 'a small rising ground surrounded on the top with a fosse'.
2 I, 199.
3 Both Gold Castle and the 'handsome square' escaped the notice of the late Mr Callander when he searched for them in 1917; see *P.S.A.S.* LIII (1919), p. 145.
4 Perthshire, 85 s.e.

closely. In the lower sunlight of the afternoon the shadow-lines of the earth-work were remarkably plain and of unmistakably Roman straightness. On 20 April 1940 I went over it on the ground and confirmed my opinion that it was Roman. The site is immediately opposite Danemark Field. When I saw it then it was under a coarse white grass and the outlines had been blurred by ploughing at some rather distant date.[1] It has now, I am told, been again brought under plough, again through the operations of war, and unless the area is promptly reserved, all traces of it will quickly vanish. As it was, though I could trace the course of the ditch continuously, the bank was only faintly visible.

There are three sides only, the Tay forming the fourth. The north-east side extends for 116 yards in a south-easterly direction; the overall width of bank (such as it is) and ditch is 20 yards, and the vertical height about 3 ft. There is no entrance-gap. The south-east side is 186 yards long and is broken at 110 yards from the south-east corner by an entrance-gap or causeway 12 yards wide. The south-west side is only about 50 yards long, the north-west end having been destroyed. At the point where this side would reach the river is a small modern stone jetty.[2]

Gold Castle was first described in 1757 by Maitland whose dimensions (180 × 122 yards) agree quite well with mine (186 × 116 yards), allowing for subsequent damage and other factors of uncertainty. My measurements would also give a circumference of 538 yards which agrees very closely with the figure of 535 given in the *O.S.A.*[3] Maitland calls it 'the Golden-castle' saying that 'in this fortress is a tumulus, out of which a considerable quantity of golden coins have been dug', thus accounting for the name. The writer of the *O.S.A.* mentions a small brook running through the fort, on the south side of which brook 'about 30 yards up from the river are the vestiges of a fortification called the Silver Castle; probably from a vulgar idea that money was hid in it'. Maitland's 'tumulus' and this 'Silver Castle' are probably to be equated with the small square marked on the Ordnance map and referred to above; its position fits the description quite well.

Of the exact age and purpose of Gold Castle fort nothing is known but it is undoubtedly Roman. It can hardly have guarded a bridge except on the hypothesis that there was an earlier bridge here before the one at 'Bertha' was built. The gold or silver coins, which might have helped so much, have

---

This was probably during the Napoleonic wars, for the writer of the *O.S.A.* (xviii [1796], p. 82) refers to 'the recent operations of the plough'.
*N.S.A. Perthshire*, p. 1169.                    3 xviii (1796), p. 82.

long ago vanished, if they were ever found; and no other finds are on record. Now that the site is once again under crops an air-photograph would reveal much and is most urgently needed.

Gold Castle stands on a plain near the foot of a hill called Donald's Bank, on whose summit can still be seen part of the Roman marching-camp of Grassy Wells, discovered by General Roy in 1771 (Fig. 13). Here is the north-west corner of the camp and this, as at Battledykes near Forfar, is the highest point in it. Grassy Wells has been fully described by Mr Callander who, with Mr Thomas McLaren of Perth, devoted much time to the restoration of its outline. As a result of their work and my own subsequent visits, combined with air-photography, it has been possible to recover the course of the north and east sides and parts of the two others, and to plot them on the 6 in. map.

Grassy Wells is a good example of what modern field-work, carried out on the ground and above it, can accomplish on difficult terrain, if maintained over a period of years. To begin with, in 1917, there was nothing but Roy's plan; the site only was marked on the Ordnance maps. Since Roy's time the face of the land has been altered out of all recognition; his farm of Grassy Wells has vanished, together with the fields round it, though their ridge-and-furrow is still plainly visible from the air (Plate XI). Consequently, it was not easy even to transfer the outline of the camp from Roy's plan to the 6 in. map. The result shows only a rough agreement with the actual outline of that part of the camp which has been recovered by other means. Until it has been possible to insert the features upon a modern map from observations made on the ground and from the air, a Roman fort or camp must be regarded as only imperfectly known and recorded, even though a plan as good as Roy's may exist. None of those concerned would, I am sure, think of claiming to have discovered Grassy Wells; but, speaking for myself, I do claim to have put it on the map.

There is no need to go again over the ground covered by Messrs Callander and McLaren whose account is published. Both they and I after them have found continuous traces of the north side running east and west through Drumshogle wood, on the brow of the hill above the Gelly Burn. This portion was pointed out to me on the spot by Mr McLaren in 1925 and I have seen it several times since. On my last visit I found it easier to follow as the wood was cut down. The north-east corner is close to the modern road, and just here is the only portion of the bank of the east side which still remains visible. It can be seen best where it is crossed by a track; and in the photograph

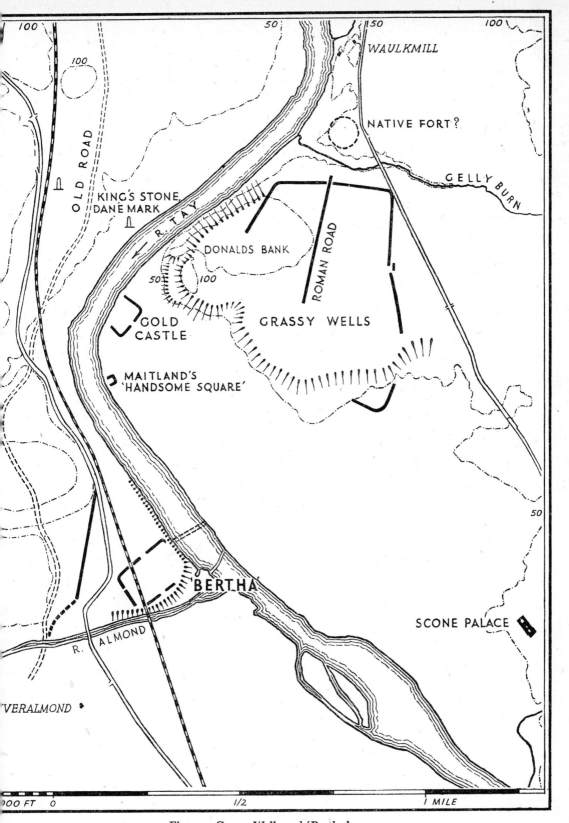

Fig. 13. Grassy Wells and 'Bertha'.

(Plate IX) it can be seen standing out against the darker background of the wood. South of this point the line of the east side was seen in the corn by Mr Callander on 10 August 1917. Mr Callander's description is not quite clear, and it must be remembered—and set to his credit—that his acute observations were made before air-photography had familiarized us with the reactions of crops to invisible banks and ditches. But it is now quite certain that what he saw was in fact the crop-mark of the ditch of the eastern side of the camp. That has been proved by air-photographs taken subsequently, one of which is reproduced on Plate X. Starting from a point on the plate $1\frac{1}{2}$ inches to the left of the upper end of the avenue, there may be seen a narrow dark line running cross-country for a distance of 600 ft.; then there is a break of about 90 ft.; then the line continues almost straight, but with a very slight curve, for another 900 ft. where it is lost in a rough wood at a point 300 ft. north-east of Sherifftown farm. This line represents the darker green corn growing above the silted-up, and therefore moister and more fertile, ditch of the camp. Opposite the gap on the outside we should look for the traverse protecting the entrance, and there sure enough it is, faint but unmistakable. (It is more clearly visible on another photograph taken at the same time.) There are no traces whatever to be seen on the ground, except in so far as one can see the crop-mark there at the right time of year.

In passing I should call attention to two other features of minor interest which the air-photograph reveals. The broad irregular lighter bands between darker are the courses of streamlets drained since Roy's time; and the broad round mark where the western one rises may be the site of the grassy wells which gave a name to the camp. Immediately to the left (west) of this is a dark circle probably marking the ditch of a round cairn or mound of the Bronze Age. For close-by, but just off the photograph, is where some Bronze Age urns, described by Mr Callander[1] were found in 1917, together with a cup-marked stone and other relics associated with prehistoric burials.

That is how matters stood up to 1941. In that year an R.A.F. instructor, Flight-Lieutenant Bradley, became interested, and in June of that year he took the photograph reproduced on Plate XI. At the top you will see the farm and wood of Sherifftown. Across the middle are the ridge-and-furrow marks of the eighteenth-century farm, with the enclosure-banks bounding the fields. Cutting into these at the top is a U-shaped dark mark revealing the south-east corner of the Roman camp. I visited the spot in May 1943, and went over the ground with the photograph. The field was under corn, and

---

[1] *P.S.A.S.* LII (1918), pp. 131–9.

it was just possible to detect slight signs of the mark, but they were so slight that without the confirmatory evidence of the air-photograph I should never have seen them at all. The curious white splash beside it was again visible and proved to be a deposit of fine silt brought by rain-wash that had collected there. I took a photograph of it from the edge of the wood (Plate XII): its eastern side, shown in the left-centre of the plate, points directly at the southern end of the dark mark seen on Plate X. Only in the wood is a gap which neither ground-work nor air-photography has been able to bridge. Nor can the remaining portions of the southern and western sides be identified between here and Donald's Bank.

The camp would appear to have been about 2800 ft. across from north to south and the north side to have been about 1600 ft. long; but it seems to have had an irregular figure.

We left the Roman road a long way back on the Gask ridge, touching it again inferentially at 'Bertha' Bridge. We catch one fleeting glimpse of it here from the air, as it crosses the middle of the camp of Grassy Wells. The cause-way can be seen also on the ground under favourable conditions, running across the ploughed field as a low broad pebbly and gritty ridge and in Drums-hogle wood, now that it is cut down, as a low stony causeway. It left the camp by the north gate, and James Knox[1] records the important observation, if such it be, that the epaulement of the traverse was 'cut through for the egress of the road, which shows the latter to have been a subsequent work'.[2] After this the road is no more seen, except for three separate fragments, one at least of which is a little doubtful. I have devoted more time and labour in the field to investigating this part of the road than to any other in Scotland, but with the most meagre and uncertain results. The general course is indicated, but the exact course not definitely marked on the Ordnance map. Chalmers, following Maitland (but in greater detail) and Roy,[3] describes the road as passing from Grassy Wells by Gellyhead, Innerbuist, Nether Collin, Drichmuir, Byres, Blairhead, Gilwell, Woodhead, Newbigging, Gallowhill, Leiston Moor to the alleged Roman camp at Coupar Angus. The writer of the *O.S.A.* gives a similar course as far as 'near Gallowhill', but he says it 'bends to the Ila at Windyedge, where the remains of another military bridge are distinctly to be traced, and the houses adjacent to which still go by the

1 *The Topography of the Basin of the Tay*, Edinburgh (1831), p. 41.
2 This is at variance with Roy's statement that this gate had no traverse and I suspect that Knox, who was no field-worker, was merely amplifying Roy.
3 *Military Antiquities*, pp. 107–8.

name of Bridgend'.[1] Roy traced the road himself in 1771 along the course described as far as Leiston Moor (now represented by the farm of Layston) where he lost it; he thought it probable that the road continued along the high ground south of the Isla, passing thence immediately north-west of Coupar Angus. The Ordnance map gives the same course as far as Gallowhill, but from there takes it through Strelitz Wood to Woodside north of Burrelton on the Perth-Coupar road where it is made to end.

We thus have three accounts to choose from, but all three agree from Grassy Wells as far as Gallowhill. Here Roy and the Ordnance Survey continue it north-eastwards by different routes; but the writer of the *O.S.A.* makes it turn northwards across the Isla. If the last was correct, the road he describes must have been a branch road leading to Inchtuthil—which must have been connected somehow with the main road. Unfortunately, I cannot locate this route on the modern map; but the remains of the bridge mentioned may perhaps be identified with a double row of stones or piles which Mr Bradley saw from the air crossing the Isla about 50 yards below the modern Bridge of Isla, during a drought in July 1941. That there was a crossing here is suggested by the fact, unknown to Mr Bradley, that exactly where the presumed bridge ended on the north-west bank of the Isla, there is a disused hollow way running north-westwards to an old lodge of Meikleour and an old road beyond. On the other hand, there is no trace of a causeway, and the crossing may be of much later date. One would have expected the *O.S.A.* bridge to be a little higher up the Isla; for a crossing of the Isla at the old bridge necessitates a very circuitous route thence to Inchtuthil, whatever may then have been the course of the Tay.

I have examined the alleged O.S. route at Gallowhill and in Strelitz Wood both on the ground and from the air on many occasions. In the fields immediately north-west of Gallowhill there are certain faint indications— a bump in the hedge 87 yards north-west of the sharp bend in the road from Gallowshade to the Collace-Cargill road, with a stony ridge continuing across the field to the south-west, called Moonshade. This is directly in the O.S. course; and somewhere hereabouts Mr Bradley saw it clearly from the air. If the alignment be prolonged it would pass close to the farm of Layston, where Roy last saw it. I am therefore inclined to accept this portion provisionally—and, with rather less confidence, the whole of the O.S. route between Grassy Wells and this point. But beyond Gallowhill to the northeast I think there has been some confusion on the O.S. map between the

1 *O.S.A.* XIII (1794), p. 536.

Roman road and a medieval track called the Abbey road, which is also marked. This is said to have been a road from the Abbey of Coupar Angus to their land at Campsie, but it may just as well be an old road from Coupar to Perth. I think that the track called on the O.S. map 'Roman road' between Woodlands and Strelitz Wood at Wellsies, continuing for half a mile into Strelitz Wood, is really the old Abbey road; if continued it would link up quite easily with the track so called in Gallowhill wood.

To sum up. All authorities agree on the course as far as Gallowhill, though no trace of the road can now be found before it reaches that place, and then only faint ones. Thence it seems that the road may have gone to Coupar Angus, possibly throwing off a branch north-west to Inchtuthil. To the two hypotheses about its course to Coupar I will add a third, my own. If the Gallowhill fragment be produced it will fall into line with a straight piece of modern road leading from Coupar to Caddam. Where this same alignment crosses the Coupar Burn at Brunty there is an old bridge with a deep traffic-rut leading down to it on each side of the valley, both in the same alignment and now quite disused. These no doubt were caused by traffic using the bridge, and together they are evidence of a much-used road, but of medieval date. Immediately below (north-west of) the bridge, however, and right on the river-bank is a large earthen mound that looks like the abutment of a wooden bridge. Is it Roman? It is evidently older than the bridge, but even so it might still be medieval. I submit that the alignment thus indicated is worth following up, on the ground and still more so from the air. At present it is no more than a working hypothesis.

# Chapter Five

## STRATHMORE: INCHTUTHIL TO KIRRIEMUIR

W E left the Roman road from Grassy Wells—or more correctly from 'Bertha'—at Gallowhill pointing towards Coupar Angus with a possible branch to Inchtuthil. We shall now visit Inchtuthil and the other Roman remains, actual and alleged, round it, and shall then proceed north-eastwards up Strathmore. There are, however, about thirty sites to be investigated along our route and off it, only eight of which are certainly Roman. Obviously there is not room to do justice to them all in the short space available if one is to devote adequate attention to such outstanding sites as, for instance, Inchtuthil. I shall perforce, therefore, be compelled to pass over most of the unproven sites, which I have described more fully at the end of the book. Some of them are ghosts which have haunted Roman Scotland for nearly a couple of centuries, and it is high time they were put to rest. Others may eventually be re-embodied by the spade or air-camera and should therefore not be passed over in a preliminary survey.

Inchtuthil[1] (Fig. 14 and Plate XIII) is situated on an insulated plateau on the north bank of the Tay in the parish of Caputh, 10 miles north of Perth, and within the park of Delvine. When I visited it in 1925 the area was mainly under grass; but it had been cultivated at an earlier date, and when I last flew over it, in 1939, I observed that it had been turned into a golf course— a measure that will no doubt have ensured the reservation of that portion from war-time ploughing. It was excavated in 1901 by the Society of Antiquaries whose Report[2] has been reinterpreted and made more intelligible by Sir George Macdonald.[3] My remarks here are based almost entirely upon these two sources, chiefly the latter. The visible remains consist of a large square enclosure whose sides were about 1500 ft. long, containing about 55 acres, a smaller enclosure called a 'redoubt' lying on the edge of the

1 The Roman fort seems to have been well known in the fifteenth century, but regarded as 'ane riche town' of the Picts, which they burnt on the approach of the Romans. See Bellenden's *Boece*, Book IV, Ch. 14 (*Hist. and Chronicles of Scotland*, 1 [1821], p. 145).
2 *P.S.A.S.* XXXVI (1902), pp. 182–242.
3 *Journal of Roman Studies*, IX (1919), pp. 113–22.

plateau to the south-east, a linear earthwork[1] 1600 ft. long, with the ditch on the south-west, cutting off the south-west projection of the plateau, on

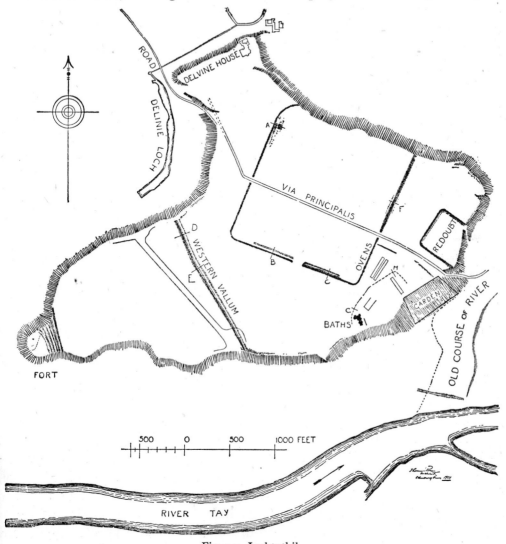

Fig. 14. Inchtuthil.

whose extreme western tip is a small promontory fort of $2\frac{1}{4}$ acres, defended by five ditches and ramparts. On the south-east side of the larger Roman

[1] This is now under cultivation. Flying over it in September 1943, Dr St Joseph observed the bank as a *white* soil-mark suggesting, on the analogy of the Vallum, turf-work, 'in which case', he adds, 'it is Roman'. It is good to have evidence of this, though I had never supposed it could be anything but Roman.

fort are two tumuli, the western one lying partly upon the bank of the Roman counterscarp and being therefore of later date. There were formerly many more, according to Pennant, and it is not unreasonable to regard them as the burial-places of the people who constructed the native promontory-fort, possibly in the Dark Ages. The Via Principalis running west-north-west through the middle of the larger Roman fort can be traced for a short distance outside it. Almost immediately after leaving the fort it makes a turn north-westwards and can be traced for 500 ft.; there is then a break of between 450 and 500 ft. where it is lost in shrubberies, but a fragment about 100 ft. long in the same alignment can be seen just south of the drive up to Delvine House, on the north-west brow of the escarpment. Here it is lost and there are no traces of it beyond this point.

Besides these remains the baths uncovered and left open after the 1901 excavations were concluded, presented in 1919 and still more when I visited them in 1925, a 'melancholy spectacle of desolation and decay'.[1] Whether they are still visible in a forest of nettles and other weeds I do not know. Perhaps they have become a 'bunker'.

The excavations in the larger fort revealed remains of timber buildings on the south-west side of the Via Principalis, and the use of red sandstone blocks in the construction of the rampart, both indicating semi-permanent occupation. This was not, then, a mere marching-camp, but 'the winter quarters of a small army, from seven to ten thousand strong. And that army was in all probability Agricola's, for the whole of the pottery fragments were Flavian.'[2] The bath-house, Sir George argued, is not likely to have belonged to the semi-permanent camp, for it is too small. He therefore associates it with a permanent fort lying to the east on ground that the river has eroded. The 'line of ditch' on the excavators' plan, he suggests, may be the annexe of this hypothetical fort. With the utmost respect for the authority of Sir George, I find it difficult to accept this explanation, for I cannot believe that the Tay can have eroded so much ground since Roman times. I should assign the baths to one or other of the groups of buildings to be described; and I should regard the 'annexe' as a small temporary camp (Fig. 15).

In the same area the excavations revealed remains of both wooden and stone barracks, whose lay-out conforms respectively with the alignment of two separate fragments of ditch on the north-east, indicative of two forts of different ages. Presumably it was to one of these that belonged the ovens which were built in the ditch of the semi-permanent camp after it was

1 *J.R.S.* IX, 121.                    2 *J.R.S.* IX, 114–15.

abandoned. It is to one of these two forts that I should prefer to assign the baths. Whatever the age of these, two facts are clear: (1) they were early, i.e. 'Agricolan (in the wider sense in which it is convenient to use that

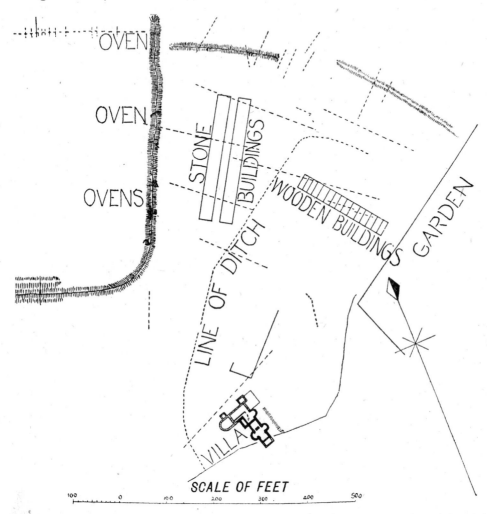

Fig. 15. Remains of permanent forts at Inchtuthil. (This figure is slightly reduced from the original plan, now in the Library of the Society of Antiquaries of Scotland.)

epithet)', says Sir George; and (2) they lasted long enough for substantial repairs to be made in one of the stone walls. Although no Antonine pottery was found on the site, Sir George regarded it as 'just conceivable' that 'the stone barracks may be as late as the Antonine period'.[1]

1 *J.R.S.* IX, 120.

I fear it is impossible to give a really clear account of a site compounded of so many uncertainties and complications, and in any case Sir George Macdonald's original account should be read for its own sake.  Its purpose was to adduce evidence for a prolongation of the Agricolan occupation of this part of Scotland after Agricola's recall in A.D. 84; and Sir George considered that this occupation continued down to at least as late as A.D. 104.[1] The evidence of excavation was subsequently reinforced by that of a coin,[2] which, when more carefully examined, proved to have been minted after Agricola's recall; and the main thesis has been generally accepted.

The Roman name was Pinnata Castra which is mentioned by Ptolemy and, in the locative form Pinnatis, by the Ravenna geographer.  The name used by Ptolemy was of course in Greek, Πτέρωτον Στρατόπεδον, and it has sometimes been translated Alata Castra.  Mr Richmond was the first to identify, and convincingly explain, the name.[3] Pinna is a military term which connotes a breastwork with parapets placed upon a rampart, and Pinnata Castra is the most precise and effective name that could be used of such a legionary fortress as this.  The name Inchtuthil means 'the meadow of Tuathal' (a personal name anglicized in Ireland as Toole).  But there is a hint, not hitherto noticed, of an older name.  A farm on the haugh across the river, immediately opposite the fortress, is called Kercock which means in Celtic 'the red fort', an excellent description of the walls of red Gourdie sandstone of which the fortress was built.[4]

Sir George Macdonald has shown that Inchtuthil was almost certainly Agricola's base before the battle of Mons Graupius, and his subsequent winter quarters.  It was also held by the Romans for a good many years afterwards.  But, while the tactical position is a strong one, strategically it is a bridgehead and open to attack from the dangerous quarter: for the Tay is on the south, the wrong side.  In order to mark out an indisputable boundary, the Roman military authorities constructed an earthwork, now called the Cleaven Dyke. This consists of a large bank, now about 30 ft. wide at the base and 5 ft. high, set equidistantly between two shallow flat-bottomed ditches, 16 ft. wide and 2 ft. deep, which lie 150 ft. apart from centre to centre (Fig. 16). The existing remains can be traced from near the farm of Hallhole

1 *Journ. Roman Studies*, XXVII, 94; XXIX, 25, n. 65.

2 *P.S.A.S.* LII, 233–4.                   3 *P.S.A.S.* LVI (1922), p. 299.

4 The Roman fort at Llandovery, Carmarthenshire, was called Tre Coch (the Red Place) from the many (red) Roman tiles found there, according to Haverfield (*Trans. Cymmrodorion Soc.* [1908–9], p. 60). A similar explanation is possible here.

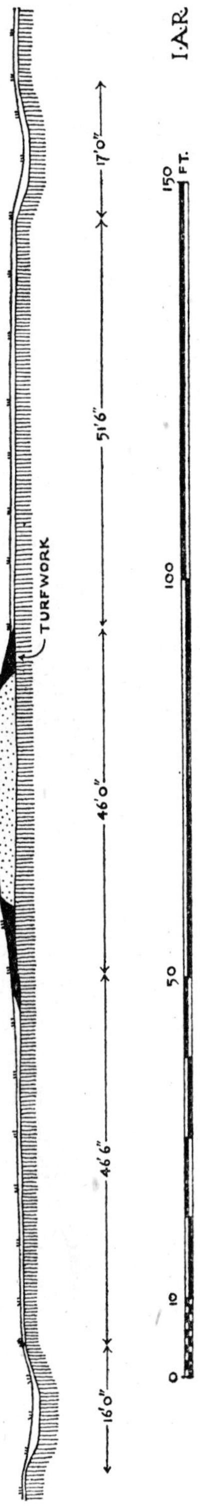

on the Isla through the North and South Woods of Meikleour, across the Perth-Blairgowrie road (near which it is well preserved and easily accessible) to the road-fork south-west of the farm of Nethermuir of Pittendriech. The total known length is 2970 yards (1·7 miles). There are two original gaps near the Perth-Blairgowrie road. There is no other earthwork exactly like it, but it may be compared with the Vallum, parallel to Hadrian's Wall on the south, of which it is a sort of inversion and whose purpose may have been similar. For both of them 'cut off, by means of their outer mounds or ditches, a broad linear strip of land'. With its exposed northern front, the fortress of Inchtuthil obviously needed some such 'artificial barrier, blazing through the forest', as Richmond says, 'the limits of Caesar's land: for such an operation *limitem scindere* was the Roman term'.[1] There is no reason to suppose that it ever continued much further westwards than its present known termination near Nethermuir, and repeated air-observation has failed to reveal any further traces of it. Allowance must be made, however, for the possibility that its course may have partly coincided with an existing road or hedge-line; and observations from the air should be made once more in May or June along the line north-westwards to Steedstalls.

The hill of Gourdie is 2 miles north-west of Inchtuthil, and is regarded as the source of the stone used for some of the Roman buildings there. On its north-eastern end is a curious affair called the Steedstalls. It consists of six stalls or recesses quarried out of the side of the

[1] *P.S.A.S.* LXXIV (1940), p. 45.

Fig. 16. Section of the Cleaven Dyke.

hill, separated from each other by a partition (Plate XIV). It has been explained as a place of concealment from which the native Caledonians watched the Romans 2 miles away, as a series of burial-chambers, and as a row of stables! Mr Bradley (25 July 1941), knowing nothing of previous descriptions, reported seeing other stalls as crop-marks round the eastern side of the hill, the whole being enclosed with and parallel to a crop-mark with rounded corners, suggestive of a Roman fort, with sides about 200 yards long. Unfortunately, all his photographs of it were unsuccessful, and I must say that the one which does show part of the stalls does not show the enclosing line. Issuing from the middle of the east side he saw a single dark line, not parallel with the plough-ridges, that suggested a Roman road. The fact that he did not recognize it as such adds weight to his evidence. A little digging would settle the matter once and for all. The site is a likely one for a fort; for it is right on the alignment of the Cleaven Dyke and well within sight of Inchtuthil; but for the present it must go to the suspense account.

Before we set our faces once more north-eastwards, there are two jokers to dispose of. The first is Buzzart Dikes or the Great Caledonian Camp, in the parish of Kinloch, 3½ miles north-west of Blairgowrie. Here, we are told,[1] the battle of Mons Graupius was fought over 4 miles of country; the natives sat down (*insederant*) in the Caledonian camp, and the Roman legions took their stand 4 miles back in front of the Cleaven Dyke, whose two-foot ditches would doubtless reinforce their courage from behind. After their defeat the flight of the natives is to be 'traced by numerous tumuli' extending along the ridge towards Blairgowrie. It was a leisurely flight, with plenty of halts for cairn-making, cremating the bodies of the dead and such-like old-fashioned ceremonies. The ramparts follow an irregular course, the southern side following close along the south bank of the Lornty Burn. Nowhere is there the slightest resemblance to any known defensive work, Roman or native, and the fact that the ditch is on the *inside* of the bank should suffice to dispose of any such idea. The Buzzart Dikes are plainly intended to keep in animals, probably deer, not to keep out humans. They are comparable with

1 *O.S.A.* IX (1793), p. 261; XVII (1796), p. 479; XIX (1797), pp. 367–71 (the Rev. Mr James Playfair); *P.S.A.S.* XXXIV (1900), p. 107. Pennant also mentions it (*Tour* [1772], 2nd ed. [1776], II, 452–3). See also *Trans. Perthshire Soc. of Nat. Science*, VII (1918–23), pp. 28–32 (plan facing p. 36). On the making of modern dikes see R. Forsyth, *Beauties of Scotland*, 1805, ii, 86. The best modern account of Buzzart Dikes is that in *P.S.A.S.* LXXVII (1943), pp. 45–8.

several others, such as Sir Allan the Durward's Deer Dike between the Loch of Lintrathen and the Isla, and may confidently be assigned to a (late?)

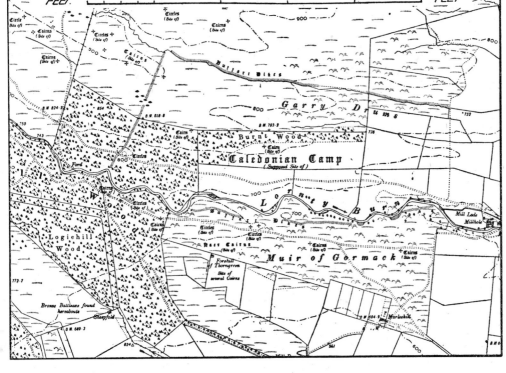

Fig. 17.  Buzzart Dikes and adjacent sites.
(*From the Ordnance Survey map with the sanction of H.M.S.O.*)

medieval date.  But we must not be ungrateful to the good minister, for not only were his speculations responsible for getting inserted on the map many cairns[1] and ancient enclosures that might otherwise have been overlooked,

1 These are marked on the O.S. map (Perthshire, 52 s.w.) as 'site of', but they are still for the most part in excellent preservation.  Some are not cairns at all but remains of habitations. The most north-westerly one on this sheet consists of an outer wall of loose stones enclosing a circular area 67 ft. in diameter, with an inner wall mostly of bigger stones (some still standing upright on the inner side) enclosing an area whose inner diameter is 32 ft.  There is an entrance-gap on the south-east.  Attached to it are the ruined walls of small enclosures. A hint of their age is given by the discovery of a bronze axe near by.  As at Luncarty, it is these remains which originated the idea of the battle, which has now become embodied in a spurious 'tradition'.

but he has also given us some valuable information about runrig cultivation and solid-wheeled carts.

The latest and best description of Buzzart Dikes is that by Messrs Childe and Graham (1943). As they say, a 'full objective account of the remains' was required, because the speculations of earlier and less scientific investigators have accorded a certain authority; and the Royal Engineers had accepted without question the opinion of the minister, calling the site the 'Caledonian camp'. There is no need to repeat here the detailed description of the course of the 'ramparts' given by Childe and Graham. It will be enough to say that 'the earthwork encloses an irregular oblong area just under a mile long on the south, and about 1470 yards on the north, by about 650 yards wide along its western margin and 470 on the eastern...the work is best preserved at its western end where it runs S.S.W. across the ridges and hollows.'

The other site is at Fortingall and has more claim to consideration, though it is certainly medieval, not Roman. A plan of it is published in Roy's *Military Antiquities* (Plate XIX), but it was not made by Roy, who states that he did not visit the site. There were two earthworks here—a 'camp' enclosing 80 acres, and a 'praetorium'. The latter is plainly a medieval moated site and consists of a squarish area surrounded by a bank, outside which is a broad wet ditch. On the south side there is an outer bank 3 ft. high in places. The north side measured along the top of the (inner) bank is 117 ft. long, the west side 96 ft., the south side 132 ft. The inner bank is 7 ft. wide on the north side and about 2 ft. high at the north-west corner. Along the inside of the bank runs a small ditch. In the south-east angle are the foundations of a round stone structure 12 ft. in diameter. The moat is 34 ft. wide on the south side which is crossed by a causeway (of doubtful age) 23 ft. wide. There is another, probably original, causeway across the eastern moat 11 ft. wide at the top which is at the level of the natural surface outside, and is 38 ft. long. Opposite this is a gap 12 ft. wide in the inner bank. There are two causeways, both probably modern, across the western moat. The moat, though somewhat silted up, is still 'wet', and was supplied with water by an artificial channel. A small bank and ditch runs north-westwards from the north-east corner, and there are others on the surrounding plain, from some of which the 80-acre 'Roman' camp may have been imagined. There is nothing Roman here, however, and every indication of medieval work, which is confirmed by the discovery, recorded by Pennant, of 'a copper vessel, with a beak, handle, and three feet'. The artificial channel or supplying the moat with water is a characteristic feature of medieval moats in England, and there is another Scottish example at Fordoun. We may safely eliminate Fortingall from the list of Roman sites.[1]

To return to the Inchtuthil district. On the farm of Hallhole where the Cleaven Dyke ends, are several conical hills of glacial origin. The westernmost, Craw Law, stands at the north-east corner of the grounds of Meikleour, at the north end of and behind the splendid beech hedge (Plate XV) beside the Perth road, on the right-hand side of this view. On its slopes are strip-lynchets, the remains of former cultivation, and on the top is a reservoir. It is an obvious place for a signal-station, and the same may be said of the others; but though one of them bears the significant name of Coin Hill, it is only on Black Hill that remains of a signal-tower have been found. This hill was excavated in 1903, under the impression that it was a disc-barrow. It was re-excavated in 1939 by Mr Richmond, who proved that on it had stood a wooden signal-tower of the Gask type (Fig. 18). The tower was surrounded by a turf bank 12 ft. wide at the base and still 3 ft. 8 in. high; it enclosed a space about 19 ft. square, with rounded corners. This was enclosed within a V-shaped ditch with the narrow square channel at the bottom typical of the Roman *fossa fastigata*. The entrance causeway is on the north side; and Richmond points out that 'the tower is so placed as immediately to survey two passages through the [Cleaven] Dyke', where, as he rightly supposes, native tracks must have passed through it. Whatever its exact connections, it must have linked Inchtuthil with the main Roman road.[2]

It will be remembered that the remains of an old bridge over the Isla have been noted both in ancient and modern times, though it is uncertain whether they refer to the same thing.[3] The site discovered by Mr Bradley is 50 yards below the existing Bridge of Isla, on the Perth-Blairgowrie road; and on a hill a quarter of a mile south of this bridge Mr Bradley saw in a field of oats, in July 1941, the crop-mark of what he believed to be a Roman fort (Fig. 19). It is situated on a flat hill-top immediately south of the Isla at its junction with the Tay, about midway between the bridge and Cargill station, on the farm of Cargill Mains. The fort, if such it be, is rectangular with rounded corners, the long axis running north-east—south-west; the

---

1 See Pennant, *A Tour in Scotland*, 1772, Part II (1776), p. 25; *O.S.A.* II (1792), pp. 449, 456; Roy, *Military Antiquities*, Plate 19, p. 134; Chalmers, *Caledonia*, I (1807), p. 174 (note); *P.S.A.S.* XLIV (1910), p. 121 (note); *Scottish Note-book* (O.G.S.C. 1925, giving measurements).
2 *O.S.A.* IX (1793), p. 506; *P.S.A.S.* XXXVIII (1904), pp. 82–7; LXXIV (1940), pp. 37–40.
3 P. 68.

marks consist of two parallel green lines representing a double ditch. The size, paced on the ground by Mr Bradley, so far as he could make it out in

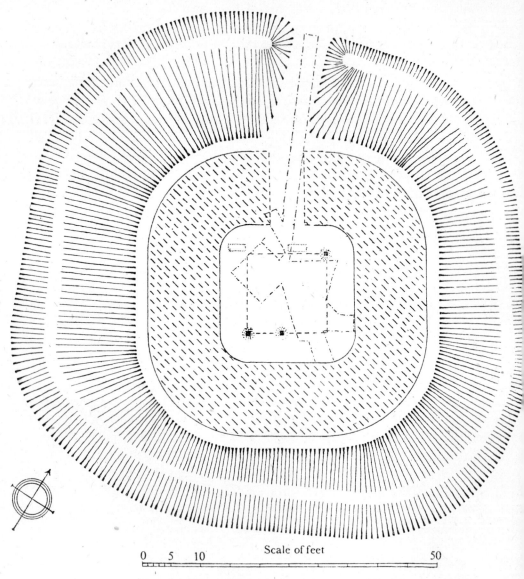

Scale of feet

0    5    10                         50

Fig. 18. Plan of signal-tower, Black Hill, Meikleour.

the stubble, was about 60 × 40 yards. Black Hill is plainly visible from it. This is the obvious place for a fort guarding a bridge, and it is tempting to accept it as Roman. The site is normal for such forts; but when I walked over the area in May 1943, I could find no indications whatever of anything, although some traces of crop-marks should have been visible in the young corn. An air-photograph taken under the proper conditions should decide the matter, and we must await some such confirmation before accepting the fort.

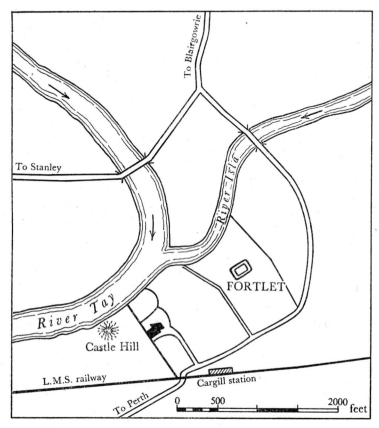

Fig. 19.  Conjectural Roman fortlet, Cargill (after Richmond and Bradley).

On the edge of the Tay immediately west of the Mains of Cargill is a fort called Castle Hill. I have never had time to visit it, but have little doubt, from the mention of an aqueduct, no doubt to fill the moat with water, that it is medieval. Richmond[1] calls it a 'large motte', but he is wrong in identifying it with Pennant's 'mount exploratory'[2] which must be Black Hill; for the writer in the O.S.A.[3] is plainly copying Pennant, with amplifications. A mile south of Mr Bradley's Cargill site, Dr St Joseph (during a flight

1 P.S.A.S. LXXIV, 40.        2 Tour, II, 452.        3 IX, 506.

undertaken in September 1943), observed what he considered to be the site of a signal-post.[1]

We can now resume our progress up Strathmore, and rejoin the main Roman road where we left it south-west of Coupar Angus. Whatever may ultimately prove to have been the exact course, there can be no doubt, I think, that it must have passed through Coupar Angus, following the low ridge that runs parallel to the Isla on the south-east, between Keithick[2] and Meigle. Just before Coupar Angus, at a sharp bend in the Isla, is the farm of Kemphill, and west of it is a low flat-topped hill, 172 ft. above sea-level. Here a 'small Roman camp'[3] or 'redoubt'[4] has been placed. I have not actually walked over the hill, but only looked at it from the higher ground to the south, whence no irregularities can be detected in its outline. But the name Kemphill may indicate some kind of an earthwork, Roman or native; and one day the corn will just as certainly reveal the secret, if there is one, to an observer from the air.

Coupar Angus has been claimed as the site of a Roman military earthwork, but the claim is unsubstantiated (Fig. 20). Maitland[5] describes it as 'an equilateral quadrangle'—more concisely, a square!—'of four hundred yards, fortified with two strong ramparts and large ditches, still to be seen on the eastern and southern sides, and on part of the northern; but the western, by agriculture, is demolished'. Roy[6] mentions it but does not commit himself to any opinion. The writer of the *O.S.A.*[7] describes it as 'nearly a regular square of twenty-four acres'. Chalmers merely repeats verbatim Maitland's account of 50 years before. In 1845 only the eastern rampart, immediately east of the churchyard, was surviving.[8] Major Bayley, R.E., who surveyed the region about 1859 for the large-scale Ordnance map, has recorded in the *Object Name-book* that the description 'Roman camp' applies to 'a raised bank, being the "eastern rampart" [of the *N.S.A.*]. It is on the course of a much frequented footpath; the sides of the bank were sloping until recently, when in the economy of agriculture they have been cut steep on either side.' I have walked over the site many times, and while

1 I am indebted to Dr St Joseph for permitting me to record this observation, of which he informed me in a letter dated 19 September 1943.
2 Not to be confused with Keithock near Brechin, the name of a marching-camp, which is spelt 'Kiethick' by Roy.
3 W. Marshall, *Historic Scenes* (1880), p. 227.
4 J. Knox, *Basin of the Tay* (1831), p. 64.
5 *History*, I (1757), pp. 199, 200.
6 Roy, *Mil. Antiq.* (1793), p. 133.
7 XVII (1796), pp. 10, 11.
8 *N.S.A. Perthshire*, p. 1142.

the existing state of the remains is such that no opinion can be formed about their age, I feel convinced that a square earthwork did formerly exist. The church and remains of the Abbey stand exactly in the middle. The east rampart, referred to by Major Bayley, is called on the map[1] Thorn Alley; it is exactly 1200 ft. long, confirming Maitland's figure. There is still a bank and the ground on the west (interior of the 'camp') is 3 ft. higher than that

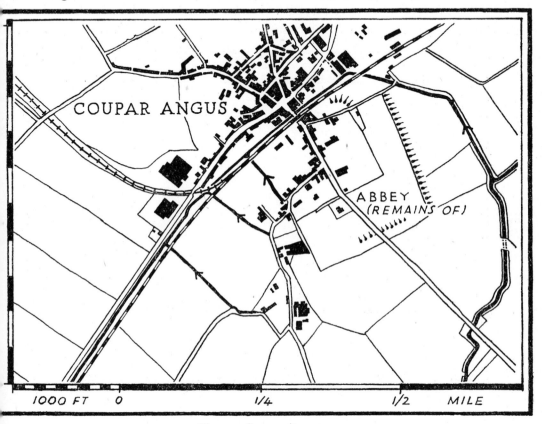

Fig. 20. Coupar Angus.

on the east. There are no remains to be seen of the north and west sides, but their former course is partly indicated by civic boundaries. The south side also has gone; the course is again indicated by a civic boundary, but 100 ft. to the north of this, and parallel to it, the map marks, by means of hachures,[2] the line of a bank which has now entirely disappeared. Possibly this second line was the second or inner of the two ramparts described by Maitland.

1 Forfarshire, 48 N.W.; Perthshire, 64 S.W.
2 These appear only on the Forfar sheet.

But there is a complication. Within this large square existing property boundaries indicate another, whose south side passes through the site of the existing Abbey ruins. The east wall of the churchyard forms part of its east side; and if this be prolonged, it will run into a raised mound whose slopes face first east and then north. The fragment, which is in a grass field behind (east of) the Strathmore Inn, just north of a lane, looks rather like the levelled round corner of a Roman fort; but it may be natural. There is no sign of a ditch. This hypothetical inner square does not seem to be referred to in

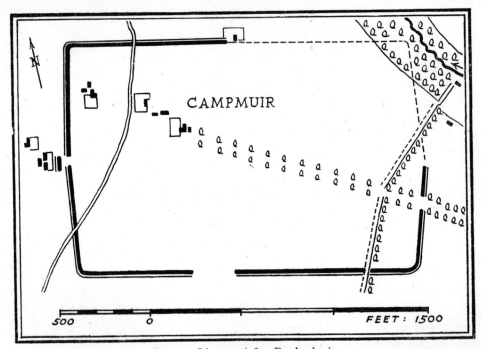

Fig. 21. Lintrose (after Roy's plan).

the older descriptions unless it should be Maitland's second rampart; but I do not think it is, for, if so, he would surely have given its dimensions.

On the whole it seems more probable that the large square delimited the precincts of the Abbey. The objects recorded as found hereabouts include nothing Roman and are, so far as one can form an opinion from them, exclusively medieval in character.[1] The recorded dimensions do not fit into any of the usual Roman categories; the shape, and proximity to Lintrose,

[1] Whetstone (*P.S.A.S.* xxii [1888], pp. 8, 147); medieval(?) bronze chape (*P.S.A.S.* xi [1876], p. 383; xxvii [1893], p. 358); more than twelve stone coffins, and some small stone figures 'representing warriors' (*O.S.A.* xvii [1796], p. 11, n.).

are against it being a marching-camp, and if it were something more permanent, surely some relics would have turned up. The most one would expect would be a fort like Strageath or 'Bertha', such as considerations of distance do certainly demand hereabouts. A very little digging would settle the matter definitely; the best places would be the flat mound behind the

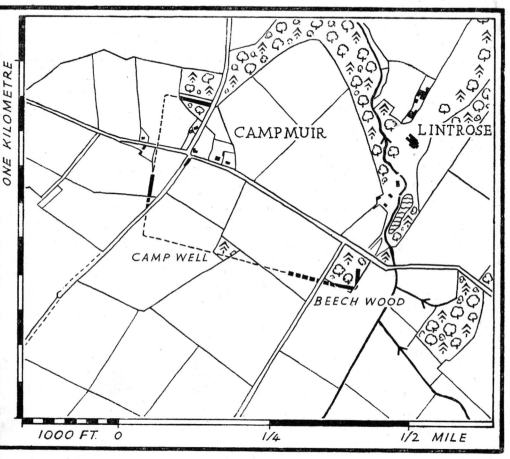

Fig. 22. Lintrose to-day.

Strathmore Inn and points in the east and south sides of the large square. The section of the ditch would be decisive, even if no finds were made; and if it was medieval, there probably would be finds.

We must now retrace our steps southwards for a little over a mile, to visit the marching-camp of Lintrose (also called Campmuir), one of the least known of its kind. It was discovered on 11 August 1754, by General (then

Captain) Robert Melville, who promptly informed Roy.[1] Soon afterwards, probably in 1755, Roy visited it and made a plan of it (Fig. 21).[2] He was able to trace about three-quarters of the outline, and commented on the fact that there was only one gate extant, in the middle of the west side, although sufficient of the other sides then survived for gates to be seen if they had been made. He gives the mean dimensions as 1900 × 1220 ft., which agrees fairly well with those one can still measure on the Ordnance map (about 2000 × 1300 ft.). When Roy made his plan there were missing only the eastern half of the north side and the northern half of the east side. There are now visible only the eastern end of the south side, and a small adjacent part of the east side, both in Beech wood; and about 300 ft. of the north side near the north-west corner, between it and the road from Campmuir to Coupar (Fig. 22). When I first visited the site in 1925 a short portion, about the same length, of the west side was visible, the bank forming the boundary between a field of potatoes and one of raspberries; and its continuation across the corner of the next field on the south as marked on the O.S. map[3] was confirmed by a band of darker green in a wheat field. But when I revisited it in 1939 the site was occupied by bungalows and gardens. There is, however, every reason, apart from this confirmation, to trust the outlines as marked on the Ordnance map, for they were put there by Bayley in 1863, who states in the *Object Name-book* (*Forfarshire*, p. 33),[4] that he did so 'from personal inspection and comparison with Roy's plan'.

The two best preserved parts of the ramparts are the extreme southern end of the east side in Beech wood, and the bit of the north side west of the Coupar-Campmuir road. At the latter point the bank is 20 ft. and the ditch 9 ft. wide; the top of the bank is about 5 ft. above the bottom of the ditch. The spot is a camping-ground of gipsies who throw their rubbish in the ditch.

The site is a curious one, for three distinct rivers flow on parallel courses but in opposite directions. The Kinnochtry Burn, on whose west bank the camp lies, rises at Collace on the north-west slopes of Dunsinane and flows northwards for 5 miles to join the Coupar Burn at Coupar only half a mile from the Isla. But the Coupar Burn then flows south-westwards for $1\frac{1}{2}$ miles on a course roughly parallel to the Kinnochtry Burn, from which it is divided only by the low ridge of Balgersho. The camp is between these two rivers, and its east side almost touches the Kinnochtry Burn.

1 *P.S.A.S.* VII (1869), p. 30.    2 Roy's Plate XIV.    3 Forfarshire, 48 N.W.
4 I am glad to say that the old *Object Name-books* of Scotland are still preserved at the Ordnance Survey.

There are several interesting remains in the neighbourhood. At Pitcur, $2\frac{1}{2}$ miles south-east of Coupar Angus, is an earth-house (called 'Picts House' on the 1 in. map) which, though neglected, is still in a fair state of preservation. It was excavated in 1878, when a Roman coin (now lost) and parts of three Samian bowls, one of the second century, were found.[1] One of the stones is cup-marked, and another, built into the north wall at C on the plan[2] has three curious engraved figures unnoticed by the excavators. It would appear to have been inhabited during the Roman advance, or at any rate not long after it. There is a sculptured cross-slab in Kettins church-yard, and a stone with a fine but rather weathered wolf carved on it stands in a small clump of trees by the north-west side of the old hillside road three-eighths of a mile east of Baldowrie.

At Auchtertyre, 4 miles east by north of Coupar Angus, is what the *O.S.A.*[3] calls 'some traces of a camp' in what is now a ploughed field. The *N.S.A.*[4] speaks of 'evident remains of a camp of square form and of no great dimensions', adjoining Crew well. The old *Object Name-book* of the Ordnance Survey (*c.* 1860) says that no traces were visible; but this was an error, for the surveyors themselves marked three of its four sides (omitting only the eastern) by broken lines; and when I visited the site in 1925 slight traces were still visible, suggesting a double ditch.[5] Each of the sides thus marked measures about 350 ft. on the map. Inside the area thus enclosed is a mound on which aspen trees grow. The earthwork is most unlikely to be Roman.

From Coupar Angus to Meigle there is little choice of route; and if our road followed the high ground north-west of the town,[6] it may be represented by the winding lane from Causeway-end—a most suggestive name—to Gartloch Bank, Middlehills, Bogside, Beech-hill, Townhead and Larghan; and the drive to Larghan is exactly in alignment with the south-west end of the field road to Wester Balbrogie. From there I suspect that the Roman road left the modern by-road and fell into the line of the main (Forfar) road at Arthurstone, following it past Meigle to Cardean. The course thus proposed from the Perth-Blairgowrie road at Byres to Cardean, a distance of 13 miles, is almost entirely hypothetical; but it is in accord with Roy's views[7]

1 *P.S.A.S.* xxxiv (1900), p. 202; lxvi (1932), p. 387.      2 xxxiv, 203.
3 iii (1792), p. 403.                                          4 *Forfarshire*, p. 559.
5 The broken lines do not appear on the second (1902) edition of sheet 42 s.e.
6 I had not overlooked this route, but it was Mr Richmond who first convinced me of its probability; since then I have not had an opportunity of looking for it on the ground. The most likely place would be the fields between Larghan and Wester Balbrogie.
7 *Military Antiquities*, p. 108.

and the other old accounts, written when actual remains of the causeway were to be seen, and it follows a persistent alignment that often coincides with existing roads and field-boundaries. I hope someone will test it on the ground.

We pass by the outskirts of Meigle, resisting the temptation to turn off into the village and see the sculptured stones,[1] and so reach Cardean, the most northerly known permanent fort not only in Scotland but in the whole Roman Empire (lat. 56° 36′ 0″: long. 3° 9′ 30″ W.). This fort occupies the point of high ground between the Isla and the Dean immediately to the north-east of their confluence. It is described on the Ordnance map[2] as 'site of Roman camp', and is in the parish of Airlie, in the county of Angus (Forfarshire), whose boundary on the Dean and Isla encloses it on two sides. Though known for over a century, the fort has only emerged gradually into full recognition. Roy mentions Cardean as the place where the Roman road probably crossed the Dean;[3] but if rumours of a fort there had reached him, he says nothing about them. The first writer who mentions the Roman fort is Knox[4] who describes the ramparts as already 'so much levelled that their dimensions cannot now be exactly ascertained'; and he expresses surprise that these 'vestiges of Roman works' had 'escaped the notice of antiquaries till within these few years'. (He also states that the Roman road passed through the 'camp', but gives no details, and I suspect that, as usual, he was simply copying Roy.) There are brief mentions in the *N.S.A.*[5] and in early numbers of the *Proceedings*;[6] but the fort was first put on the map, in the literal as well as metaphorical sense, in 1861 by Colonel Bayley, R.E., to whose interest in archaeology we owe so much. Although traces of the fort were then still visible, they were evidently not clear enough to be actually marked but only the verbal description quoted above inserted. Along the northern edge of the plateau is added the record of 'earthen vessels, etc. found',[7] and these are more fully described in the *Object Name-book* as 'earthen vessels, human remains, iron implements and coin'; and other

---

1 These are exhibited in a building close to the churchyard, where they were found. Their abundance indicates that Meigle was a place of importance in the Dark Ages. Mr Ralegh Radford was the first to show that there is historical evidence for this: 'The existence of the school [of stone carvers] centred at Meigle in the late eighth or first half of the ninth century must be connected with the court of the kings of Gowrie, the house of Ferat, which figures so often at this date in the list of the kings of the Picts.' *Antiquity*, xvi (1942), p. 16.

2 Forfarshire, 42 N.E., 43 N.W.    3 *Military Antiquities*, p. 108.

4 *Basin of the Tay* (1831), p. 83.    5 *Forfarshire* (1845), p. 679.

6 *P.S.A.S.* ii, pt. 2 (1858), p. 246: v, pt. 2 (1865), p. 349.

7 Sheet 42 N.E.

objects were said, by Mr H. J. Fitchie, of Deanfield, to have been found in the fort. Just outside the fort, between it and Wester Cardean, the map[1] marks the site of a 'weem' or earth-house, which was partly uncovered in Bayley's presence. (The site was marked by a low mound on which grew a tall pine tree, visible on the air-photograph, but cut down just before my visit on 14 October 1939.) Close-by there was found a Roman sword and some tiles. The sword seems to have passed from Mr Fitchie to Lord Talbot de Malahide who pronounced it to be Roman. It is described as a 'straight iron sword'. The exact site of its discovery was not known, but we may take it that it was pretty close to the position on the map marked by the words. The discovery of tiles here speaks unmistakably of a bath-house.

Between Bayley's visit in 1861 and my own in 1925 no one seems to have seen the site; I recorded then that there were no surface indications visible. But I had it on my list of sites to be looked at from the air, and we included it on our flight to Aberdeen on 7 June 1939. The moment I saw it I recognized it as quite certainly a Roman fort. The broad crop-mark with its rounded corner and entrance-gap in the middle of each side is certainly Roman. Only one photograph unfortunately, was taken, and it is not good enough to publish: perhaps it was taken from the wrong angle. I can, however, assure you, having seen it myself, that the outlines *seen* were extremely clear and unmistakable. The ramparts run from the steep cliff above the Dean, hidden in the trees on the south, to that above the Isla on the north; there was none on the other two sides. Within the area of the fort various faint lines tantalizingly indicate streets and buildings that more favourable crops and a better photograph might reveal in startling detail. That they are Roman is shown by the fact that they run parallel to the north-east rampart.

Through the middle of the fort runs the Roman road, broken where it passes through the defences, and broader for the first sector within. It evidently continued south-westwards, and there are remains of it on the sloping side of the plateau, above the bridge at the mill. It would seem to have crossed the Dean Water at this bridge and to fall into the line of the Coupar Angus road at Cardean Lodge; but south of the river there are no traces of it. And what are we to make of that other straight line on the air-photograph diverging from it and running direct to Wester Cardean? I think it must be of modern agricultural origin, for it crosses the lines of the fort diagonally, and the five trees along it suggest that at some time it had been a field-boundary.

1 Sheet 43 N.W.

Beyond this there is nothing till we come to Westmuir, 6 miles north-east of Cardean, in the parish of Kirriemuir. The course of the Roman road here, generally associated with the name of the farm of Reedie, was first described in 1757 by Maitland[1] as follows: '...It appears again on the southern side of the village of Riddy; and entering the moor, becomes the common road for about the space of half a mile, pointing to the town of Kenymoor [Kirriemuir], about a mile to the eastward. This is the last time I could discover its course.' Roy saw it on his westward journey back through Strathmore in 1771 'between Reedy and Killymoor; pointing to the southward of the first, and to the northward of the last-mentioned place'.[2] The accuracy of Roy's observation of the alignment is strikingly confirmed by the short length of 860 ft. marked on the O.S. map,[3] which has just this direction. For this we again have to thank Bayley—from his description of it in the *Object Name-book*[4] the road appears to have been only faintly visible. When I first inspected the site in 1933 the field was under grass and I could see nothing. On a second visit in October 1939 the field was arable and I saw a very stony patch almost exactly on the continuation of the alignment, beside the road to Auchindory; while at the other end, where the marked course meets a lane at Westmuir, in a recently cleaned drain I observed much 'stoniness' exactly on the alignment marked. From the air, also in 1939, I noted faint indications only. But the evidence, though slight, is cumulative and consistent, and I accept it without hesitation.[5]

Between Cardean and Westmuir I think the Roman road may well have followed the same, or nearly the same, course as the modern road as far as Lendrick Lodge; but although I have been over this route I have found no traces of it, nor could Sir Torquil Munro, the owner of Lindertis, or his overseer, Mr Macintosh, throw any light on it. We spent a pleasant after-noon searching for it in the wood called on the map Lendrick Bank; we were looking not only for the road but also for a 'small earthen tumulus surrounded by a circular fosse' which the writer of the *New Statistical Account* says was to be found 'in the old firwood of Landrick'.[6] This (as Dr St Joseph had pointed out to me) seemed, from the description, to be a candidate for a

---

1 *Hist. of Scotland*, p. 200.     2 *Military Antiquities*, p. 108.     3 Forfarshire, 37 N.E.
4 I speak from memory here, not being now able to consult it and not having copied the description.
5 While these pages were in proof an air-photograph (Plate XVI) taken by Mr Bradley has confirmed the course here described. I wish to thank Mr Bradley for it.
6 *N.S.A. Forfarshire* (1845), p. 679.

signal-post, and therefore a clue to the road. Both my companions considered that 'the old firwood of Landrick' should refer to the wood now called Lendrick Bank on the map; but, with all due deference to their intimate knowledge of the estate, I am inclined to think it may have referred to what is now a moorland on high ground north-east of Lindertis. Here are many enclosure-banks (but no plough-rigs) and there is an open growth of firs, suggesting a former plantation. A made road runs along the ridge in a south-south-westerly direction; and between a southward bulge in the road and the letter 'd' in Top of the Fields (Wood) on the 6 in. map I was shown a round mound said to have been 'the meeting-place of the court or market' —no doubt a 'law'.[1]  I suspect this is really the tumulus of the *N.S.A.*, though I did not see any ditch.

Maitland[2] was certainly wrong in taking the Roman road by Castleton, midway between Meigle and Glamis. No doubt he was misled by the existence there of 'a strong fort of an oblong form, about the length of one hundred yards, and breadth of sixty, fortified with an exceeding high rampart and deep ditch, which, from the great appearance of ruins, I take to have been a considerable Roman fortress'. It had already been described by a writer in 1728 in Macfarlane's *Geographical Collections*[3] when it was called the Castle-hill of Castletown and was 'good pasturage'. The moat is wide and fed by a stream. Dr Christison visited it and has published a plan and description.[4] I have also seen it both on the ground and from the air; from above, a patch of old rig-and-furrow is plainly visible a little to the north, confirming its undoubted medieval age.

To return to the Roman road. At Westmuir it points north-eastwards a little to the north of the town of Kirriemuir, but there is a gap of 2 miles where it is lost. Its next and positively final appearance is in Caldhame wood north of that town where there is a fragment of just under three-quarters of a mile (3750 ft.), for the knowledge of whose existence I am indebted to Mr Richmond. It consists of the usual low broad causeway, which starts in the plantation on the south-west side of the road (containing the house called Woodside); it passes through the south corner of Caldhame wood and after crossing a footpath falls into line with another which runs up on it for 1250 ft. Continuing in the same alignment it meets the Kirriemuir-Cortachy road at a point 200 yards south of the north-east corner of Caldhame wood,

1 See p. 152 below.               2 *Hist. of Scotland*, p. 200.
3 I, 278.                         4 *P.S.A.S.* xxxiv (1900), p. 53, fig. 4.

which is at a cross-roads.[1] Then it is lost, and I could find no further trace of it. The causeway is cut by the banks enclosing Caldhame wood itself and by other banks in the wood, and must therefore be older than these. It has no bounding banks beside it, nor does it run parallel to the boundary of the wood or any of the banks in it. It ends quite abruptly at each end, and has no apparent connection with the existing lay-out of roads and fields. For these reasons I think it must be older than any modern period to which it might otherwise have been assigned, and I accept it as almost certainly authentic—the most northerly known piece of Roman road in the Roman Empire. Let us hope that the owner or the people of Kirriemuir will label it accordingly in some conspicuous place, and thus help to preserve it for posterity. But perhaps they had better first get Mr Richmond to dig and make sure.

[1] Two hundred yards south-west of this point, in a field-boundary north of the road, is a standing-stone 6 ft. high, on a slight (natural?) mound. Its west face is covered with artificial pock-marks about 1 in. apart—a feature unique in my experience.

# Chapter Six

## STRATHMORE: KIRRIEMUIR AND OATHLAW
## TO STONEHAVEN

IN tracing the course of the Roman advance through Scotland it may be assumed that the first line of penetration is indicated by marching-camps; and that the forts and the road itself were made at a later date. The larger marching-camps may therefore be assigned to Agricola himself in A.D. 82–4, and the other works to his successors, probably his immediate successor, during the next two decades. Hitherto in our progress the marching-camps, with the exception of Dalginross, have all been on or very close to the line subsequently adopted for the road and forts. But if the road-fragment north of Kirriemuir is genuine, it can hardly have passed within less than 2 miles of the next marching-camp, that of Oathlaw, and may have left the one at Keithock nearly 3 miles to the south-east; and there is the marching-camp of Kirkbuddo, whose exact age and purpose are doubtful, far away to the south. For convenience of description, therefore, I shall deal first with these marching-camps, and then go back and follow the hypothetical course here adopted for the Roman road.

All these three marching-camps (together with a fourth, Lintrose) were discovered by Captain Robert Melville[1] on those memorable days in August 1754, when he was staying at Panmure, whither he had gone of set purpose to discover them. A fellow-guest told him about Kirkbuddo over the dinner-table, and next day he went there and 'to his great joy', which all field-workers will understand, found it. On 20 August he rode from Panmure to Brechin (14 miles) before breakfast, discovered the camps of Keithock and, later in the day, Oathlaw, dined with an old army friend at Kirriemuir, and slept at Coupar Angus, having ridden well over 40 miles. Lintrose was found the next day. In four days he had found four camps; even his friend and fellow-worker Roy only found three during all the time he was engaged in this part of Scotland. There was nothing like this in the whole of the

---

1 For further information about him see 'A biographical sketch of General Robert Melville of Strathkinness, written by his secretary'; with notes by Evan W. M. Balfour-Melville, B.A. *Scot. Hist. Rev.* XIV (Jan. 1917), pp. 116–46. He was born 12 October 1723, and died 29 August 1809.

nineteenth century, which has hardly a couple of sites to add; it was not equalled until the twentieth when the aeroplane introduced a somewhat unfair form of competition.

The marching-camp of Battledykes (Oathlaw) is 3 miles north of Forfar, between the South Esk on the north and the Lemno Burn on the south

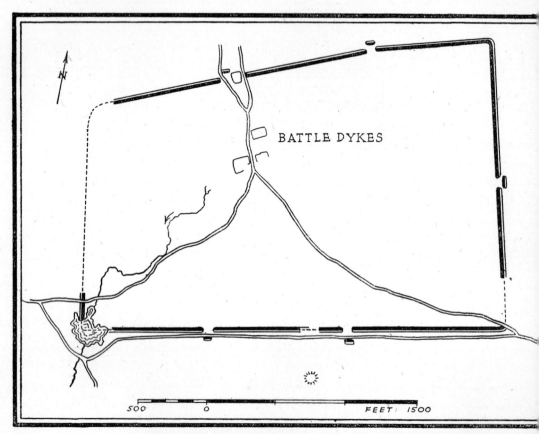

Fig. 23. Battledykes (Oathlaw). (After Roy's plan.)

(Fig. 24). It is 1950 ft. across from north to south and about 3000 ft. east to west, giving it an area of about 130 acres.[1] In Roy's time (1755) three sides were almost entire and part of the fourth remained. Four gates were 'very distinct', and the fifth visible but the traverse levelled (Fig. 23). 'On the south side of the camp there is a very large tumulus or cairn, composed of loose stones, and placed in such a manner as to render it hollow in the middle,

1 Roy (*Military Antiquities*, p. 66) gives it a mean length of 2970 ft. and a mean breadth of 1850 ft., with an area of 3,780,952 sq. ft. His plan is on Plate XIII.

thereby forming a sort of parapet, which surrounds it at top.' Maitland[1] speaks of a farmer ploughing up a road within the camp; he identifies this with our main Roman road.[2] An account by the Rev. Mr Jameson of Forfar, dated 23 April 1785, is printed in *Bibl. Top. Brit.*, vol. v, and also in Gough's *Camden*, iv (1806), pp. 152 ff. The writer speaks of *two* ramparts with a ditch between (Maitland also mentions this possibility, but states that he could not check it, as agricultural operations had made it impossible). Speaking of

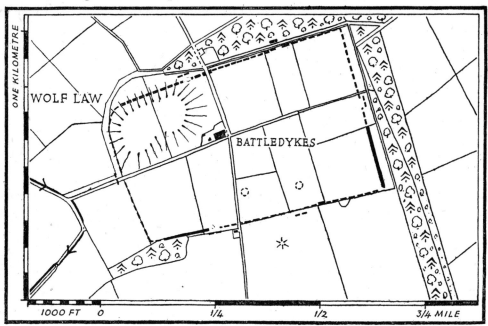

Fig. 24. Battledykes (Oathlaw) to-day.

Roy's tumulus Jameson adds the information (which is also given on his accompanying plan) that from it 'a causeway juts out southwards towards the rivulet [Lemno]. It has been carried on for sixty paces, is ten paces in breadth, composed of earth and stones; but the design has not been carried on. It terminates in a place where there has been a druidical temple; as we there find three large stones, fallen over, in the order and of the size of those that are generally found in these remains of heathen antiquity. This tumulus is vulgarly called Centry hillock.' Inside the gate is the base of a tumulus called 'the King's house', of a form that has been 'somewhat square', and

1 *Hist. of Scotland* (1757), p. 200.
2 An air-photograph taken in 1947 shows two dark parallel lines running from the farm of Battledykes to a point just N. of the S.E. corner of the camp.

one of the stones composing it 'seemed to have been hewn'. There was another tumulus within the camp, 'a little within the gate on the east side, nearly on a line with it'. The bottom of the camp ditch was alleged to be still between 10 and 12 ft. below the top of the rampart in places, and the overall width of both between 14 and 15 paces.

Near the south-east corner, outside the camp, Mr Jameson saw part of another enclosure, with no visible ditch. The north side ran parallel to the south rampart of the large camp, extending slightly to the east of its east side, then turned southward for 200 paces, then westward for 120 paces, and was 'lost in the [plough] ridges'.

The writer of the *N.S.A.*[1] adds nothing to these descriptions except a record that 'in trenching over some part of it lately, there were found some small urns...a coffin of stone' and 'an iron instrument resembling the flourish of a flint or steel'.

From these remarks it is plain that, as at Grassy Wells, there was a pre-historic burial-ground on the site. To the same period I should attribute the 'causeway' from the tumulus, and of course the tumuli themselves.

After 1845 no one, so far as I am aware, visited the camp or at any rate published any description of it till I went there in 1925. During nearly a century and a half ploughing had almost completely levelled the ramparts, though they could so easily have been preserved as field-boundaries by making a few very slight adjustments of the lay-out. Only a little over 500 ft. of the rampart of the south side, towards its west end, is still visible, exactly on the Ordnance line, 16 yards north of the fence, continuing for a short distance along the north edge of the wood, which used it as a boundary. The ditch was just visible as a crop-mark in the stubble, when I visited the site in 1939. Nothing else of the south rampart or of the small enclosure outside its south-east corner was to be seen on either visit. The whole of the ditch on the east side was seen, the north part in 1925 and the south part in 1939, as a crop-mark exactly on the course shown on the map.[2] At the point where a newly-cleaned field-drain, also a field-boundary running slightly east of north from the farm of Battledykes, intersects the east ditch, a section of part of the latter was visible in 1939, and showed a filling of lighter reddish soil mixed with stones.

Hardly any traces of the rampart or ditch on the north and west sides were visible on either occasion; but in 1939 I found the traverse covering the eastern of the two entrances. It consists of a mound in the edge of the

1 *Forfarshire* (1845), p. 297.          2 Forfarshire, 32 S.E.

wood on the north side of the road, exactly at the point where the word 'gate'[1] is written in the 1903 edition of the 6 in. map. There is a pine tree on the east end of the mound. On the north side the ditch is plainly visible, the mound is 20 yards long, and ends on the west opposite a field-gate and ash-tree. West of this there is a bump in the road-hedge where the line of the rampart crosses it south of a cottage (the 'Cotter toun' of the plan in *Camden*).

The north-west corner of the camp is on a natural hill called Wolf Law, and here a bare patch, without clover-stalks, was visible from below on the west, indicating the course. The inclusion of this hill must have been deliberate; it could have been quite easily avoided by placing the whole camp a quarter of a mile to the east of where it is. We saw the same thing at Grassy Wells (Donald's Bank).

The smaller enclosure is interesting. It seems to have been older than the large one, for otherwise surely it would have been placed in the south-east corner of the latter?[2] As it is, the plan, as published, suggests that the makers of the camp used the ditch of its north side for their own south side. There was another such at Cleghorn and one at Kirkbuddo, but no traces survive of any of the three. I see no reason to doubt that they were all of a kind, and Roman. The one at Kirkbuddo, as we shall see, had a traverse across the entrance.

About midway between Forfar and Carnoustie, and 7 miles south by east of the camp at Oathlaw, is the marching-camp of Kirkbuddo, also called Harefaulds and in the seventeenth century Norway dykes (Fig. 25). It was the first of the four discovered by Melville, and it is most reluctantly that I must say that it had already been mentioned, after a fashion, by Gordon,[3] not at first hand but quoting an unpublished manuscript of Commissary Maul written in Latin 120 years before his time. Maul, however, quotes the usual

---

1 Meaning, as the type of lettering shows, Roman gate. The word appears on the edition of 1903, but not on that of 1927 which I was using when I discovered it; and it was only later that I noticed it. My rediscovery was therefore made quite accidentally, and was not prompted. The word has unaccountably been omitted from the edition of 1927.
2 Knox (p. 122) says it was within it, but this is incorrect, as Jameson's plan and description plainly show—if it is this to which Knox is referring?
3 *Itin. Sept.* (1726), p. 154. On p. 33 Gordon refers to Commissary Maul's 'Manuscript History, written about 114 years ago'. Written as would thus seem about 1606–12, it would be the oldest topographical account of Scottish antiquities based upon some actual inspection of them, if we exclude Buchanan and his medieval predecessors. Maul certainly recorded remains which are mentioned nowhere else and have since been destroyed, such as the tumuli at Barry and the cist-burial near the Cross of Camus. But, to judge from Gordon's extracts, the valuable first-hand records would appear to have been mingled with much valueless

rubbish about the Danes, derived from Buchanan, and tells us nothing whatever of the slightest value about the camp itself, nor does Gordon. Melville was the effective discoverer and to him the honour is due. He and his friend and contemporary Roy come into the stuffy room of eighteenth-century antiquarianism like a breath of clean, fresh air. They tower over their contemporaries and many of their successors as did Bede over the other monkish chroniclers and hagiographers.

In Roy's time the camp was almost perfect, all six gates and all but part of the north-east side being preserved. About the middle of this side and just outside was the farm of Harefaulds, and here there is no visible trace of the ditch and banks for a distance of 500 ft., nor of the northern of the two entrances. There is also a gap, of about the same width, in the south-west side near the north-west angle, occupied by a swamp, and Jameson[1] was probably correct in thinking that here the rampart was never built. Outside, at the south-east angle, was a smaller enclosure consisting of two lines of rampart and ditch smaller than those of the camp and each 150 paces long. Two of the three sides were shown on Roy's plan and Jameson's, and there was an entrance in the middle of the south-east side covered by a traverse.[2] It occupied the highest ground, but has vanished completely. In the middle of the large camp were four large mounds made entirely of earth. Mr Jameson was told by his surveyor that when these mounds were removed 'he had seen a considerable number of pieces of old shoes among the earth, and that they were all square-toed'. Several hundreds of old shoes were found in the fort of Bar Hill on the Antonine Wall.[3]

When I first visited the camp in 1925 I could trace the whole course of the north-west side and its traverse by a line of thistles growing over the ploughed-up ditch, which itself could also be seen as a slight depression. In 1939 I could see nothing though the field was still under grass. Except for the

speculation. The original manuscript was said to be 'at Edinburgh' in 1871. A copy then preserved amongst the muniments of the Earl of Dalhousie at Brechin Castle was seen by Dr John Stuart and is thus described by him (*Hist. MSS. Commission Report*, II, 186, col. 2): '*De antiquitate Gentis Scotorum, contra Anglorum calumnias* [*et*] *mendacia: authore magistro Roberto Maule, Officiali seu Commissario S. Andree. Fideliter descript. ex autographo penes Comitem de Panmure, manu propria authoris.*' This manuscript copy is unfortunately inaccessible; the present owner cannot find it amongst his archives. It would be desirable that, when possible, it should be consulted and selections from it published. The foregoing account is based on information kindly supplied by Dr C. A. Malcolm, of the Signet Library; and I have also to thank Mr Fred Ferguson, Town Clerk of Brechin, for his help in connection with it.

1 Gough's *Camden*, pp. 153, 180.    2 Ibid. See plan between pp. 152 and 153.
3 Macdonald, *Roman Wall*, 2nd ed. (1934), p. 451.

gap mentioned the greater part of the north-east side could be traced either in 1925 or 1939. Most of the south-west and south-east sides fall within the area of an open fir wood and are, or were in 1939, very well preserved,

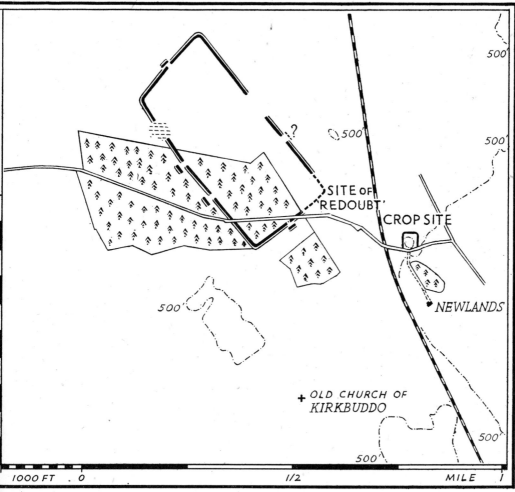

Fig. 25. Kirkbuddo.

including the three traverses which are not marked on the O.S. map.[1] The top of the bank is here about 6 ft. above the bottom of the ditch (Plate XVII). The traverse covering the southern of the two entrances is 60 ft. from the middle of the entrance, which itself is 47 ft. wide. The bank of the traverse is 42 ft. long. The overall width of the bank and ditch of the south-east side near the south-west corner is 25 ft., and just north of the modern road it is

1 Forfarshire, 45 N.W.

7-2

30 ft. The entrance and traverse are still preserved immediately south of the roadway. The entrance is 48 ft. wide, and the traverse is 40 ft. long. A modern drainage ditch with a small bank follows the line of the rampart and is continued across the entrance. (This adaptation occurs also in the north side of Cleghorn camp, which is also in a wood.)

From the railway bridge on the east I saw in 1939 (17 October) a crop-mark in the stubble which I was able to photograph and measure (Plate XVIII b). It indicates the ditch of a rectangular enclosure situated immediately north of the road at the point where the lane from Newlands comes in. The western side is 67 paces long, the northern 52 and the eastern 43 paces. It was not possible to see whether the corners were rounded and there was no sign of any entrances. It is another obvious case for an air-photograph.

The name Kirkbuddo was connected by Skene[1] with Buite, a Munster saint who died A.D. 521. Buite was granted a fort (castrum) by the king of the Picts and built a church in it. The old church of Kirkbuddo is one-third of a mile south of the Roman camp, near a spring; stone graves were found just outside and there are two carved slabs, one with a cross on it, now lying amid the ruins, but neither of them appears to be earlier than the medieval period. Watson[2] is inclined to accept the association with Buite, through a diminutive from Buiteoc or Buitheoc. The known facts about Buite form a consistent whole except for the fact that the church is outside the camp. One is tempted to suggest that an older one may have been built inside the camp and another built later on the present site near the well. But there is no evidence for this theory.

The Roman camp of Keithock (Fig. 26) was on a site $2\frac{1}{2}$ miles north-north-east of Brechin, in the angle between the Aberdeen road, to the south-east, and the Edzell road, to the west, which crossed its west corner. It lay between the Cruick Water, a tributary of the North Esk, on the north and the high land of Logie Pert on the south. It was one of the two discovered on 10 August 1754 by Melville.[3] The camp was variously called Black Dykes, Battle Dykes and War Dykes. Even when discovered it was half obliterated by cultivation. Roy's plan of 1755 shows three-quarters of the north-west side, with a traverse in the middle, about 650 ft. of the north-east side

1 *Celtic Scotland*, i, 134.                    2 *Celtic Place-names*, p. 313.

3 In 1954 will fall the bicentenary of these great discoveries. Could it not be celebrated by a pilgrimage to the sites on the actual days (Kirkbuddo, 8 August; Keithock and Oathlaw 10 August; Lintrose, 11 August)? There are of course many other things to see in the vicinity of Brechin and Coupar Angus that could be included in the itinerary. Such a pilgrimage would revive public interest and thereby contribute towards preservation of the remains.

(forming the north-west part of that side), and almost the same length, rather fragmentary, of the south-west side. The Ordnance map[1] indicates by a broken line the portions of the three sides marked on Roy's plan. It is a fairly safe assumption that the shape was similar to that of the other marching-camps. The length of the only side measurable, the shorter one, on the north-west (1300 ft., Roy) compares fairly well with the corresponding sides at Kirkbuddo (1100 ft.), Lintrose (1250 ft.), Ardoch (1280 ft.), Cleghorn (1200 ft.), Torwood (1280 ft.), Silloans, north side (1220 ft.), Bellshiel (about 1110 ft.); the average length of the other (long) axis of these seven camps works out at 1884 ft., ranging from 2350 ft. at Kirkbuddo to 1640 ft. at Bellshiel. Now the writer in the *O.S.A.*[2] considered the original length ('from the best information I can learn') to have been 'almost one half of a Scots mile' (=2964 feet), extending from the north end of the ward of Keithock, to the Law of Keithock on the road from Brechin to Aberdeen. Knox[3] concludes that the length was 'about 1900 ft.' The distance from the north corner as marked on the O.S. map to the Aber-

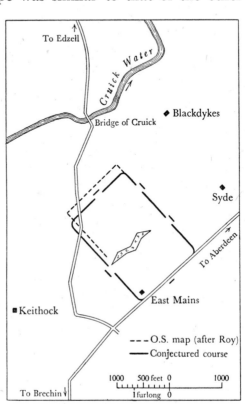

Fig. 26. Battle Dykes, Keithock.

deen road is about 2220 ft. I am not at all convinced that the north-west side as marked on the O.S. map is correct; it was almost certainly transferred from Roy's plan and not inserted from any ground measurements; and that plan has hardly any common points with the existing topography except the road, which has been straightened, the house called Wardend of Keithock, and a single corner of a field. Measuring from these I should replot Roy's plan differently, making his north-west side follow the line of the field-boundary indicated on the O.S. map by a slip of wood with a well in it (marked 'W.'); and I should shift the south-west side about 150 ft. south-westwards. This would have certain advantages. It would make the south-west side pass

1 Forfarshire, 27 N.W.     2 XXI (1799), pp. 123–4.     3 *Tay Basin*, p. 90.

through a crop-mark I saw in the clover in 1939[1] and reduce the presumed length of this side from about 2220 ft. to about 2000 ft., thus bringing it nearer both to Knox's 1900 ft. and the average figure mentioned of 1884 ft.

When I first visited the site in July 1925, it was under corn and I could not examine it properly. When I went over the ground carefully in October 1939, I thought I could see remains of the ditch of the north-east side, at the south-east end where it had already been obliterated in Roy's time. The photograph (Plate XVIII a) shows a marked sinking of the field-level as it approaches the wall, a feature that occurs nowhere else and demands some explanation. The field-bank parallel to it seems to incorporate the original rampart of the camp.[2] (This portion is 700 ft. long, starting from the Aberdeen road at bench-mark 245·8.)

The south-east side of the camp would, in the scheme here suggested, run along the Aberdeen road to East Mains of Keithock. There are no visible traces of rampart or ditch along the road, but I did see what might possibly be remains of the traverse bank, marked by a lime tree immediately to the north-east of some new houses built on the south-east side of the road. (The actual point is 800 ft. south-west of bench-mark 245·8; it falls almost in the middle of the side, as restored.)

The dimensions of the camp as thus restored, measured on the O.S. map, are about 2000 ft. by about 1400 ft. It will be interesting to see whether air-photography confirms the proposed rectification of the plan. It may well reveal the south-west side, which falls in the open fields whichever course is adopted, and some of the traverse ditches; but the three other sides, according to my restoration, could not be revealed by crop-marks as they coincide with modern boundaries and the road.

The next site is at Fordoun, 14 miles north-east of Brechin and 11 miles from the marching-camp at Keithock. There were originally two earth-

---

1 This ran north-west—south-east for a few feet only; it was immediately north of a field-boundary running from opposite Keithock Lodge to the south-west point of a zigzag strip of woodland 800 ft. north-west of East Mains of Keithock. This crop-mark was noted on the map at the time without any knowledge that it would subsequently fit so nicely into the readjusted plan proposed now, four years afterwards, and on other grounds.

2 That the north-east side followed the course indicated is proved by the observations of 'the intelligent Colonel Imrie', recorded by Chalmers (1 [1807], p. 176, n. a), that 'upon the north-east side a new boundary fence...runs in the direction of the old wall'. His measurements for the sides (395 × 292 yards) do not agree at all with Roy's, and the last remark in the passage quoted by Chalmers needs elucidation. I take it to mean that the fence coincided with the course of the rampart of the camp.

works here. One was first described by Melville as 'very distinct remains of a Roman castellum, at present planted with firs, about 300 yards east from the House of Fordoun—we paced it and it was about eighty in length and forty in breadth'.[1] This earthwork still survives intact, and we need not therefore encumber the story with the descriptions of earlier writers. It is marked on the Ordnance map[2] as a 'Roman camp', but it is plainly medieval, the moat being wide and wet, and fed by a stream entering it at the north-east corner. There is no rampart on the inside of the moat, but some traces of an outer one. In the older accounts this figures as the 'praetorium' of the Roman camp, from which one would infer that it lay within the ramparts of the other; but Knox[3] thought it lay outside. The writer of the *O.S.A.*[4] says there were then 'still the vestiges of a Roman camp. The wall and ditch, which surrounded the praetorium, are very distinct, which shew it to have been an oblong square.' In 1799[5] there was an 'extensive Roman camp' near the mansion-house of Fordoun whose remains were 'pretty complete till about fifty years ago. Since that time a great part of them have been levelled and the ground brought into cultivation. Parts, however, of two of the sides still remain; these vestiges run at right angles to one another, and seem to have composed the west and north sides of the camp. The Luther-water, which is here only a rivulet, ran formerly through the west side of this camp; and on the east side of it there are several springs.' The writer then proceeds to describe the 'very complete Roman fort, which is supposed to have been the *Praetorium* of the West Camp'. Forty-six years later the same writer described the camp again. He reveals the fact that some of the information quoted above was given to him, in his younger days, by 'old people who could trace to him a considerable part of the outlines of the camp, which were most extensive, and had been defended by triangular forts,[6] at the different corners, by outposts, and by a deep morass at the lower extremity... these outworks have now been levelled, and the morass has been

---

1 *P.S.A.S.* LXXIII (1939), p. 249: quoted from General Melville's papers by Sir George Macdonald.

2 Kincardineshire, 24 N.E.  3 *Tay Basin*, p. 99.

4 The Rev. Mr Alexander Leslie, *O.S.A.* IV (1792), p. 498.

5 *Caledonia*, I, 177, n. *d*; Chalmers here quotes 'from very minute descriptions and mensurations by the Rev. James Leslie of Fordoun, and the Rev. Mr Hutton of Edzell, which were made in 1799'. Nearly half a century later the minister of Fordoun, now Dr James Leslie, contributed to the description of his parish in the *New Statistical Account* (*N.S.A. Forfarshire* [1845], pp. 67, 85).

6 Does this imply *two* camps, one superimposed on the other and cutting the corners off?

turned into a dry and very productive field. In trenching that morass, the heads of several Roman spears were found, one of which is now in the possession of John Carnegie, Esq., Redhall. A gold ring, similar to what we are told the Roman knights wore, was also found; and a number of bones have been dug up in various places near and at a greater distance from the camp.'[1] The last finds were made in stone cists and were therefore native burials and irrelevant.

From these accounts certain facts emerge. Somewhere on the low ground of the Luther valley west of Fordoun House was an earthwork, two at least of whose sides met at right angles. It was defended by 'outposts' which may have been the banks of traverses; for that was how they were formerly regarded and described.[2] At the 'lower extremity', probably towards the south, was a morass, now drained. The area enclosed was extensive. I think we may decide that a strong *prima facie* case has been made out for a Roman marching-camp which air-photography will one day reveal. Field-work on the ground is unlikely to be productive, and my own very slight examination of the ground in 1939 revealed nothing, nor did local enquiries elicit any knowledge. But, remembering that were it not for Roy's plan it would be quite impossible to locate the marching-camp at Keithock, or even to be sure that it was Roman, we need not be discouraged by the absence of any visible remains.

Our next halting-place is at Stonehaven, a harbour, or at least an anchorage, that might possibly have been used by the Romans. Whether so or not, the Roman army that made the three or four camps further north must certainly have passed very near it; for here at long last the mountains reach the sea. Here, on a plateau spur called Arduthie, between the Urie and the burn of Farrochie, the site of a 'camp' is marked on the Ordnance map[3] in lettering used for Roman remains. It is mentioned in Gibson's *Camden*, II (1722), p. 1257, in Macfarlane's *Geographical Collections*[4] and in *Archaeologia Scotica*.[5] The *O.S.A.*[6] speaks of 'vestiges of a Roman camp [evident] a few years ago, though they are now defaced by the improvement

1 *N.S.A. Kincardineshire* (1845), p. 85.

2 Thus a writer in Gough's *Camden* (IV [1816], p. 151) calls the traverse banks in front of the entrances of the Roman camp at Raedykes 'redoubts'; and Gordon (*Itin. Sept.* 1726, p. 42) called the traverses of the large marching-camp at Ardoch (which he did not comprehend) 'out-scouts'.

3 Kincardineshire, 15 S.E.                          4 I (1722), p. 250; III, p. 237.

5 I (1782), pp. 565 ff; II (1822), pp. 300, 302; III (1831), p. 46.

6 XI (1794), p. 215.

of the ground'. A writer in Gough's *Camden*[1] locates the site more precisely as 'situated on an eminence with a precipice to the north and about a quarter of a mile from the sea'. The *N.S.A.*[2] speaks of 'remains of a camp, more distinctly Roman [than Raedykes]' as 'to be seen some years ago'. Since then there has been nearly a century of oblivion. To-day there is nothing to be seen in the glebe of the manse. Agriculture and 'improvements' had already done their work of obliteration before the railway embankment was constructed. A low round mound, 20 yards in diameter and about 1 ft. high, stands on the point of the promontory. The site is not wide enough for anything but a very small fort; for the plateau is only 600 ft. across at its widest (western) end and narrows rapidly. There can never have been a marching-camp at this exact spot, and a native fort seems more likely to account for the descriptions. It is an unsatisfactory ending to a long journey!

It is also, perhaps, a little tiresome to be obliged to return and pick up the Roman road which we have by now almost forgotten—the more so as its very existence is unproven. Personally I cannot think it ended anywhere short of some definite objective such as is offered by the geographical situation of Stonehaven, where a fort seems postulated.

Before Mr Richmond told me about the fragment in Caldhame wood, I adopted for working purposes the hypothesis that the road followed a more southerly course, passing a little to the south of Tannadice and Careston,[3] thence by Keithock to the Brechin-Aberdeen road and along it by Luther Bridge and Laurencekirk to Stonehaven; and I examined this route cursorily but without any success. Since seeing the Caldhame fragment, I should assume a more northerly course by Shielhill Bridge, Wellford, Tigerton (near Kirkton of Menmuir), Edzell, Inch, Bog Mill (near Fettercairn), Auchcairnie and thence by Fordoun House to the modern main road and Stonehaven. Along this route forts should be looked for at river-crossings, particularly at Shielhill Bridge where a medieval castle guarded the ford of the South Esk, at Wellford over the North Water and near Edzell, where the North Esk is crossed.

1 I, 151.      2 *Kincardineshire* (1845), p. 249.
3 At Nether Careston 'there was found an ancient causeway, about thirty feet broad and of considerable length. It was constructed of rough whin-stones, as closely laid, the farmer remarked, as were the stall floors of his own stables' (*P.S.A.S.* II [1859], pp. 193-4). But this is not really evidence of a Roman road, for such fords are unknown along the course of Roman roads in Scotland, where wooden bridges are more likely to have been made. For paved fords in England, see *V.C.H. Kent*, III (1932), 139, Plate XXX (paved ford at Stream Farm, Iden Green, Benenden).

Yet another line that would be worth investigation is that of the old road from Fettercairn to Fordoun and Stonehaven. This road runs along the foot of Strathfinella Hill, passes northwards through the village of Fordoun, crosses Herscha Hill (where it was called the Picts' road in the eighteenth century),[1] thence to Chapelton where it turns north-east and goes through the Mains of Inchbreck, Tannachie and Tewel, passing close by Malcolm's Mount to Stonehaven. This route has the advantage of avoiding the steep-sided ravines of the Carron water and its tributaries.

I have not yet had an opportunity of examining these routes on the ground. They are therefore merely working hypotheses, unsupported by any real evidence. In passing I would remark that the construction of working hypotheses is not only a fascinating game but also a practical necessity which in several instances has led to discovery. It is the only possible method of advance when evidence fails, for one cannot search every field on foot over a large stretch of country.

It remains to dispose of four 'camp-followers', as one might call them, which have dogged this route since the eighteenth century. The first is a small native fort, said to be vitrified, called on the map[2] Green Cairn, and situated 1⅜ miles south-west of Fettercairn, just south of the Edzell road.[3] It is first mentioned by Maitland[4] who calls it a 'beautiful Roman fort' 66 × 36 yards in size. Gough[5] duplicates it under the names of Fettercairn and Balmain. Chalmers had it examined by one of his collaborators whose careful description is published.[6] There can be no question here of anything Roman, and even if Maitland's site at Balmain should prove to be distinct, it sounds more like a medieval one.

Green Cairn is apt to be confused with another native fort called Green Castle on the east bank of the Devilly Burn, 2¼ miles north-east of Fetter-cairn. Chalmers had it surveyed and published a plan of it,[7] and another, copied from the O.S. map,[8] was published by Christison.[9] Like Green Cairn and Kincardine Castle it is also called Finella's Castle. I would take the opportunity of pointing out that this attribution, and the vast majority of

---

1 Chalmers, *Caledonia*, I, 149, on the authority of the Rev. James Leslie.

2 Kincardineshire, 23, s.w., s.e.

3 I have inspected this, but so far as I can remember, I did not see any superficial traces of vitrification. I assume that Chalmers, or his informant, was correct in identifying Maitland's fort with Green Cairn, though Maitland's distances do not fit it. But neither do those given by Chalmers!

| | | |
|---|---|---|
| 4 I, 200–1. | 5 IV, 163–4. | 6 II, 178. |
| 7 I, facing p. 178. | 8 Kincardineshire, 23 N.E. | 9 *P.S.A.S.* XXXIV (1900), p. 61. |

the others, can be directly traced to the inventions of the older falsifiers of Scottish history, especially John of Fordoun, Hector Boece and George Buchanan; and that they have no traditional value whatsoever. The older writers—one cannot dignify them with the name of historians—invented their facts to explain the forts, cairns, cists, and standing-stones that they saw scattered over the countryside. Some of these inventions may have had a local origin and even have been current in the district; but they arose *to explain observed facts*—the forts, etc.—and were not the orally transmitted record of actual events. Such so-called traditions and legends are all historically valueless.

The third site is a bank in Drumsleed Wood immediately south-east of the village of Fordoun, at the top of the steep eastern slope of 'the Den'. It is called 'earthwork' on the O.S. map[1] and consists of a low bank with a ditch on the west 400 ft. long. This bank forms the western boundary of a medieval arable field, whose ridges, 10 yards broad, run off eastwards at right angles.[2] It is thus an exact parallel to the miscalled 'Roman camp' at Guynd.[3] Even in the eighteenth century the true origin of this bank was already forgotten and it was called 'the Scotish camp', which Knox[4] magnified into a large 'British strength'. Dr Christison was puzzled but rightly concluded that the remains were not suggestive of fortifications.[5] It would be difficult to find a better example of the untrustworthiness of so-called tradition which turns a ploughed field into a 'Scotish camp' within a century or two of its disuse.

The last site is on Black Hill, south of Stonehaven harbour, overlooking Strathlethan Bay. Though marked as a 'camp' on the O.S. map[6] it consists merely of two sides of a small rectangular enclosure whose banks are obviously enclosure-banks of modern origin and could serve no defensive purpose whatever. It is said to have been the site of the encampment of Colonel Morgan when he besieged and took Dunnottar Castle in May 1652.[7] If so the besieged must have had a quiet time, as it is a mile distant from the Castle.

1 Kincardineshire, 24 N.W.
2 Another excellent example of these cultivation-ridges is to be seen in Tollmuir Wood, immediately north of the Brechin-Forfar road, between Finavon and Nether Careston. The ridges are 16 yards wide and a furlong in length, and there are at least two groups running at right angles to each other. The wood has gone.
3 P. 138 below.                          4 *Tay Basin*, p. 100.
5 *P.S.A.S.* xxxiv, 108.                  6 Kincardineshire, 16 s.w.
7 O.S. *Object Name-book*, parish of Dunnottar (1865), p. 57.

# Chapter Seven

## STONEHAVEN TO THE MORAY FIRTH

STONEHAVEN lies at the north-east end of Strathmore, actually just beyond it. North of Stonehaven the apex of the mountain triangle reaches the sea, dividing Eastern Scotland into two parts and, at a later date, separating the Northern from the Southern Picts. On a hill 4 miles north-west of Stonehaven is the Roman marching-camp of Raedykes. Sir George Macdonald[1] has written so complete an account that I can do little more than summarize it here. Later on I shall give my reasons for believing it to be the site of the battle of Mons Graupius.

The first mention of Raedykes is in Maitland's *History*.[2] Twenty years later it began to attract the attention of 'the curious'; but during the nineteenth century hardly any notice seems to have been taken of it. In 1914 Sir George Macdonald surveyed it and carried out excavations at certain points, to determine the course and character of the defences (Fig. 27). The plan is most irregular, to suit the terrain, but conforms to the orthodox rules in having opposed gates protected by traverses. The view (Plate XIX) shows the north side, looking north-east at the middle point of that side. Much the most interesting feature is the strengthening of the defences in the direction of expected attack, namely, the two northern corners and most of the east side. Here the ditch was V-shaped, about 15 ft. wide and 7 ft. deep; and the rampart was higher and broader than elsewhere. 'The ground', says Sir George,[3] 'along which the eastern side of the defences (P-Q) runs, slopes gently from north to south. Immediately in front is a stretch of flat, open moorland.' This, I observed when I visited the site in 1939, curves round to the north-west towards the hills of Curlethney (806 ft.) and Meikle Carewe (872 ft.). The top of the former is three-quarters of a mile north by west, and of the latter $1\frac{1}{4}$ miles north-west, of the north-east corner of the camp. Within the area of the camp is Garrison Hill (628 ft.). On the south and west this hill slopes rather steeply, and the defences were accordingly not so strongly made. This weakness may have been compensated by the construction of a formidable rampart of earth running for 580 ft. parallel to the south side at a distance of 800 ft. south of it. It has a deep ditch on the

1 *P.S.A.S.* L (1916), pp. 318–48.     2 I (1757), p. 202.     3 P. 335.

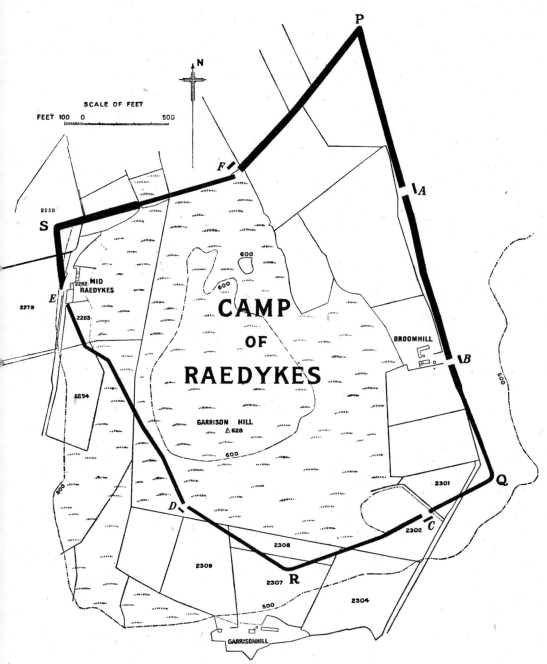

Fig. 27. Raedykes.

south-east side, in which to-day an artificial drainage-channel runs. It lies in a narrow wood with a road along its north-west side, and is marked on both the older (eighteenth-century) plans and on the Ordnance map[1] where it is called 'earthworks'. There is no evidence of its age, and it is strangely unmentioned by Sir George in his description. It will be remembered that there was a linear earthwork also at Inchtuthil. I have no doubt that it is Roman; it would help the defenders to break up an attack if one should be delivered from this quarter.

One would not of course expect the marching-camps to be connected by means of roads, for the latter were later constructions. But as the roads and forts often followed the line of the first advance, one naturally looks for them in the vicinity of the camps. No forts are known north of Cardean, and there is no evidence of any road beyond Kirriemuir. I think that a terminal fort will eventually be found near Stonehaven, and it is doubtful whether roads or forts were ever made north of this point. There is no trace of any road near Raedykes. But an army advancing northwards from here would follow the open watershed, threading its way along the bare slopes between the bogs and passing between the hill of Strathgyle and Eddieslaw, and thence along what is now a minor road by West Brachmont and Carrackstane to the Dee (Fig. 28). Here, immediately north of Tilbouries, is an old ford and on the broad hill above is the Roman marching-camp of Normandykes. It was first mentioned in the *Old Statistical Account*,[2] when the area was mainly heathland. The writer regarded it as a Norman work; but he observed the rounded north-east and south-west corners (which he calls 'half-moon work'). Chalmers[3] published a valuable plan made by Captain Henderson of the 29th regiment, which shows the greater part of the north side and the northern half of the east and west sides as intact. There are two entrance-gaps in the north side about 600 ft. from each of the two northern corners, but no traverses are shown. A traverse *is* shown, however, opposite the entrance-gap in the middle of the east side. Chalmers records that Colonel Shand visited the camp in February 1801, and informed him 'that the profiles, and other dimensions of the ditch and rampart, appeared to be the same as those of the camps at Glenmailen, and Urie [Raedykes], at Battle-dykes, and other camps in Strathmore'. Professor Stewart of Aberdeen agreed with this opinion. The size was stated to be 938 yards (east and west) by 543 yards (north and south). The whole of the southern side was already

1 Kincardineshire, 15 N.E.                    2 XVI (1795), p. 380.
3 I, facing p. 125.

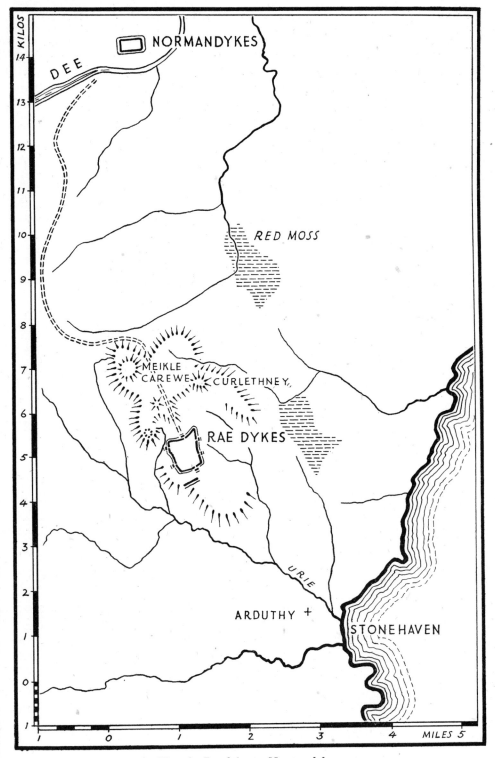

KILOS

DEE

NORMANDYKES

RED MOSS

MEIKLE
CAREWE
CURLETHNEY,

RAE DYKES

URIE

ARDUTHY +

STONEHAVEN

MILES 5

Fig. 28. Raedykes to Normandykes.

then destroyed, though apparently still traceable, as the course is marked on the plan.

The outlines are marked on the Ordnance maps[1] and form a rectangle about 2900 × 1600 ft.[2] No really convincing remains can be seen on the surface, but the north rampart is no doubt represented, for its eastern part, by the bank bounding the wood on the north. The whole of the western side, all except a tiny part of the southern and the greater part of the eastern, are in cultivated land and should be revealed by air-photography under suitable

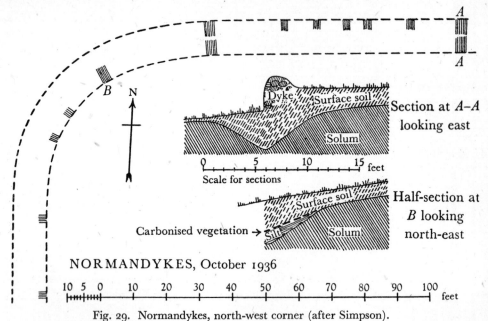

NORMANDYKES, October 1936

Fig. 29. Normandykes, north-west corner (after Simpson).

crop conditions. The Roman character of the work, already apparent from these earlier observations, has been conclusively proved by excavation (Fig. 29).[3]

From Normandykes to Glenmailen, the next certain camp, is 26 miles. The obvious marching-route would lead to the Don valley at Kintore, and

1 Aberdeenshire, 85 s.w., s.e.

2 The east side is a few feet longer than the west. These measurements agree quite well with Chalmers's, (2814 × 1629 ft.), but his area (80 acres) is much too small, unless Scottish acres are meant, and Captain Courtney's of 107·5 (*P.S.A.S.* vii, 393) is no doubt correct. Captain Courtney used Captain Henderson's plan to identify the camp and inserted it on the large-scale Ordnance map which he was constructing (*P.S.A.S.* vii, 388).

3 Reproduced (by kind permission) from Professor W. D. Simpson's *Province of Mar*, which had not been published when these paragraphs were composed.

here, at just the right distance—11 miles—what was claimed, I think correctly, as a marching-camp was located in 1867–8 by Captain E. H. Courtney, R.E., who, like Melville before him, was looking for what he expected on *a priori* grounds to find.[1] The clue was provided, after a long and fruitless search, by an obscure pamphlet (which I have not been able to consult) called '*The Early History of Kintore*, by a Kintore loon' (Mr Alexander Watt) who died about 1865 and saw the camp at the very beginning of the nineteenth century. It was then called 'Deer's Den'; the rampart was about 18 ft. wide and 6 or 8 ft. high and the ditch between 8 and 10 ft. wide. The camp was of 'an oblong square form', and included a greater part of the upper or west part of the town-land of Kintore, which was then almost entirely moorland, though the east part had even then been demolished by cultivation. Partly with the aid of crop-marks, Captain Courtney[2] was able to trace the whole of the north and west sides and about 300 yards of both the south and east sides, as well as to locate the north-east and south-west corners, but he failed to find the south-east corner (Fig. 30). The area enclosed was 110 acres. No entrances or traverses were found, though looked for. The west side has a slight re-entrant angle at the point where the modern road to Springburn crosses its line; this is about 780 ft. south-east of the north-west corner, and just where one would expect an entrance. It will be recalled that the north side of Raedykes had just such a re-entrant angle and that the entrance was placed at it. There is indeed a certain resemblance between the two camps generally, the dimensions of whose sides are similar. The sharp and deliberately protruded north-east corner of Raedykes corresponds to the similarly sharp protruded north-west corner of Kintore; in each case the purpose was to include high ground in the 'dangerous' direction. One would expect excavation at Kintore to reveal a similar strengthening of the defences in this north-west angle.

1 Edward Henry Courtney was born 6 August 1836, obtained a commission as Lieutenant in the Royal Engineers 31 July 1855, and was a Major in 1872. He took part in the China War, 1858–60, and was at Malta in 1870. He was Professor of Survey at Cooper's Hill College, Staines, from 7 July 1872 to 31 December 1887, when he retired as Major-General. In 1906 he was Governor of the Military Knights of Windsor and was made C.V.O. He died at Gerrards Cross, 21 June 1913. I am indebted to Colonel Sir Charles Arden-Close, formerly Director-General of the Ordnance Survey, for the above facts which he kindly obtained for me from the Secretary of the Institution of Royal Engineers at Chatham.
2 His paper in *P.S.A.S.* VII, 387–94 (Plate XLVIII), read 10 February 1868, is apparently the only published reference to this camp, apart from the pamphlet just mentioned.

The site is undulating and varies in height between 160 ft. near the south-east corner (whose exact position was doubtful) and about 250 ft. at the north-west corner. On the north is the Bridgealehouse Burn, on the south

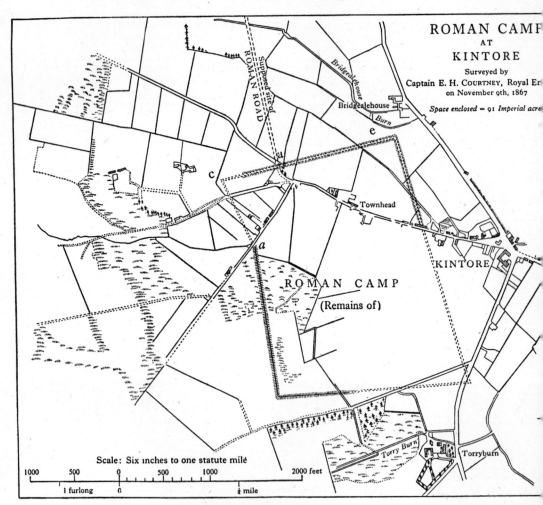

Fig. 30. Kintore, plan (after Courtney).

the Torry Burn, on the east the river Don. The outlines so carefully traced by Captain Courtney were apparently recovered too late for incorporation on the Ordnance maps,[1] the survey of which is dated 1864–5. They can, however, be exactly plotted from his plan.[2] Having done so I walked over the whole area on 13 May 1943, full of hopes which were not realized

1 Aberdeenshire, 64 N.E., 65 N.W.        2 P.S.A.S. VII, Plate XLVIII.

Nowhere could I detect the faintest swelling in the ground or any crop-marks (though it was rather too early in the season for these). Most of the area is under cultivation and air-photographs should reveal the course without any difficulty, if taken about June or July.

Captain Courtney states[1] that a brother officer of his had found 'the supposed track of the Roman road from a point near the village of Kintore northwards towards Inverurie, but he had failed in tracing this road south-wards to the river Dee'. The road does not appear on the map and is not mentioned elsewhere, and it is not at all likely to have been Roman. It must have been a supposed continuation of this road that was inserted, on Captain Courtney's authority[2] on sheet 54 N.E., along the line of straight field-walls running north-west from Brandsbutt near Inverurie. I looked at this, but the line did not look Roman, nor could I see the trace of any road at all there. Some of the best men have erred and strayed along 'vicinal ways'; even 'the late judicious Colonel Shand' was misled by one such called the Maiden Causeway leading to a native fort on Mither Tap.[3]

Three other portions of alleged Roman roads prove on examination to be parts of one and the same road for which an early but non-Roman origin seems indicated. Parts of it are called on the Ordnance map[4] 'Lawrence road', explained in the *N.S.A.*[5] as so called because it led to St Lawrence Fair at Old Rayne. No doubt it did, but I suspect the fair followed the road. I have not been over the whole course of the road but only parts of it. On the map it seems to connect with an old highway leading from Old Aberdeen by Parkhill, Fintray, Kinmuck and Harlaw to Old Rayne. Thence it goes through Kirkton of Culsalmond and along the western slope of Tillymorgan, over the Ythan divide (where it was called 'supposed site of Roman road' on the map of 1873) to the Deveron and Rothiemay. It was in fact the main road from Aberdeen to the north-west.[6]

1 *P.S.A.S.* VII, 389.
2 O.S. *Object Name-book*, parish of Inverurie, p. 36: signed by Captain Courtney, 30 November 1866.
3 I have not seen it, but as marked on the 6 in. map (Aberdeenshire, 53 N.E.) it is plainly not Roman. Macfarlane mentions it (*Geogr. Collections*, I [1724], p. 18) and gives the story of its alleged origin (which is quite entertaining). For the Maiden Causeway, see Chalmers, *Caledonia*, I, 149, and *N.S.A.* XII (1845), pp. 570–1, 734.
4 Aberdeenshire, 35 S.E.                                  5 XII, 731.
6 There are other portions of road in this district that have been claimed as Roman, at Pitcaple (45 S.W.; *N.S.A.* XII, 570; *Object Name-Book*, Chapel of Garioch [1867], p. 35) and by Cairnhill in Culsalmond (*N.S.A.* XII, 426). I have not seen them, but do not think they will prove to be Roman. See also pp. 140–3 below.

8-2

None of the alleged Roman roads in Aberdeenshire which I have inspected has yielded any evidence of being so, and I very much doubt whether any of the remainder will. No published evidence has established their claims to be Roman.

Having thus disposed of the alleged Roman roads, we come to our last certain Roman site, the marching-camp of Glenmailen, the most northerly point ever known to have been reached by a Roman army (Fig. 31). It lies near the source of the Ythan, about 8 miles east of Huntly, and midway between it and Fyvie. On this breezy upland, high, remote and inaccessible, one can understand the uneasy feelings of the Romans as they advanced ever further into the endless hostile land, and surveyed from Raedykes and from here, first the illimitable prospect of tree-fringed moorland, and then beyond the sea yet another line of mountains fading away over the distant skyline.[1] One can understand their feelings without 'imagination's artful aid' if one has conducted one's own advance on a bicycle in the pleasant month of May, pushing it through snowdrifts several feet deep along the road to Glenmailen; and one can sympathize with Agricola's anxiety not to 'spread the war' over such a region when the summer was over. Modern roads present difficulties, even in the so-called summer; and we know that Agricola, or his successor, had not even a Roman road to march along.

The Roman camp at Glenmailen was discovered by Shand in 1785 or 1786. Some time afterwards he made a plan, which, when Sir George Macdonald wrote his account of the camp, was supposed to be lost.[2] It has since turned up at Perth,[3] and is reproduced on Plate XX. When Sir George wrote, Glenmailen, which appears as Plate LI in Roy's *Military Antiquities*, was the only one of these plates for which he could find no original. It is satisfactory that this deficiency is now removed. It is of no great moment whether this newly found plan is the actual one from which the engraver worked or one of the 'many copies' which Shand says were made. I think it is the actual one, because 'Roman Camp' has been altered to 'Camp Ground' and there are other erasures bringing it closer to the published title. What *is* of importance is the fuller and more accurate information

---

1 *Trepidos ignorantia caelum ipsum ac mare et silvas ignota omnia circum spectantes* (Tac. *Agric.* ch. 32). 'By Jove,' said Agricola to Tacitus, 'that fellow Calgacus was right!'

2 *P.S.A.S.* VII, 28; L, 354.

3 In the City Museum, where the archives of the Perth Literary and Antiquarian Society are kept, and where it was shown to me in May 1943 by Mr McLaren, whose willing help in this and many other matters I wish gratefully to acknowledge.

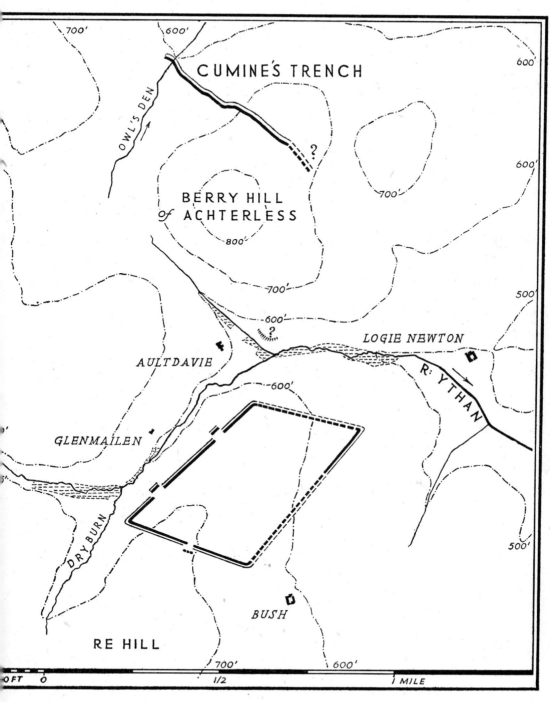

Fig. 31. Glenmailen.

contained on it. Shand had already called attention to the errors of the published plan, particularly in the spelling of the place-names. The newly found plan shows that these errors were very numerous. But there were also serious omissions. The newly formed patches of arable land, or 'grounds', shown on the original, were left out; so too was the enlarged plan of the entrance and traverse (A) in the south side. The nicely rounded south-west corner is turned into an acute angle. The south side is incorrectly copied and so are the entrenchments (W) on the north-west slopes of Tillymorgan. The ditches beside the road in the south-west corner (V, X, Y) representing the traffic-ruts of the older unmetalled road, are omitted. The section through rampart and ditch is marked Æ suggesting that it was given as typical of the defences at these *two* points, in the north-west and south sides; on the published plan it is labelled A, and badly copied. For all these mistakes not General Roy but his editors are, of course, responsible; for the engraving was made, and his great book published, after his death.

An interesting confirmation is given of Sir George's suspicion[1] that the name Re-dykes, sometimes given to Glenmailen, has no basis, for it does not appear in the original, but only in the published, title. The original is there stated to be 'by Theodore McRonald, May, 1789'.[2]

I have so far said nothing of the camp itself as it actually is. Before doing so it will be as well to examine the plan of 1789 and see what its condition was then.[3] The approximate dimensions of the sides in feet are as follows: north side, 1711; south, 1934; north-west, 2790; east, 2529. Taking the means they give an area of about 111 acres, which agrees quite well with the 'something more than ninety Scotch acres' of the published explanation (=113 imperial acres). I prefer these figures to Sir George's which gave him an area of about 122 acres.[4] When tested against some of the surviving remains as marked on the Ordnance map,[5] the accuracy of the older plan is completely vindicated. We may therefore confidently transfer some of the other details to the Ordnance map. We find that the north-west side extended

1 P. 352.
2 I wish to thank Dr Malcolm, of the Signet Library, for his help, unfortunately without results, in trying to find out something about Mr McRonald. He was probably an Aberdeenshire surveyor, but no information about him can be discovered.
3 The north point on this plan and that in Roy both aim considerably to the west of true north. Sir George Macdonald described the sides as they appear on the plan in Roy, but I think it better to speak of the south (for s.w.), north (for n.e.), east (for s.e.) sides, retaining n.w. for the fourth, as these are more nearly correct.
4 P. 355.                                    5 Aberdeenshire, 27 s.e.

about 200 ft. further north-east than is marked on the Ordnance map. The northernmost of the two entrances in the north-west side comes at the other (south-west) end of the marked portion, and indeed the gap in the rampart is just visible here on the ground.[1] Coming to the north side we have a fixed point in the north-east corner which is still preserved (Plate XXI *b*), but the side itself was practically invisible on the ground. As marked on the 1789 plan, it is not quite straight but curves slightly inwards. On the east side both the maps mark only some 800 ft. at the north end, which, if produced, hits the east end of the south side. Of the south side (Plate XXI *a*) which, like the north-west, was complete in 1789, only the western half survives and is marked on the Ordnance map, the other half being continued as a field-boundary.

The 1789 plan carefully marks the intakes or patches of cultivated ground reclaimed from the moorland as they then existed. They show that the south and west ramparts were then entire, as they were when the *N.S.A.* was written in 1845.[2] Sir George, led astray by the minister's compass-points, which are the correct ones, misinterprets his statement to imply that 'the state of matters in 1845 would seem to have been very much the same as that which prevails to-day'.[3] On the contrary, to-day only half the southern and less than a quarter of the north-western sides are preserved, and that very imperfectly. I infer from the minister's statement that in 1845 the old patch-work cultivation was still in force, and that the modern lay-out, as shown on the present map, was introduced at some later date; for it was this new system of cultivation, with its complete alteration of the field boundaries, which reduced the ramparts to their present condition.

I am tempted to go yet further and ask whether, in the portions of rampart selected for obliteration by the first cultivators we may not find a clue to an original difference in their strength, just as at Raedykes. The weaker portions would naturally be the first to go, and the strongest the last to survive. On general grounds of position one would expect the north-east angle to be made strongest, and in fact the north-east corner is still of formidable bulk. A strip of cultivation is seen from the old plan to avoid the northern angle (as also does another strip just outside the camp). But it had already obliterated all the rest of the east side. The excavations of 1913, which were rightly directed mainly towards testing the outline and nature of the camp, throw no light

---

1 I noted this gap on the ground before ascertaining, by measurement, where it fell on the map. The bank of the covering traverse is also visible and is about 70 ft. long.

2 XII, *Aberdeen*, p. 286.                    3 P. 356.

on this point, and they preceded the interesting revelations at Raedykes.[1] But it is unfortunate that no graphic record of the results was included in the report, and no new plan; for lack of this the exact course of the east side, which was ascertained, cannot now be plotted.

To-day the whole area is divided up into fields, whose boundaries incorporate the whole of the south side and a third (the north part) of the east side. These portions of the rampart are still fairly high and well preserved. The whole of the north-west rampart can be traced on the ground as a stony mound. The southern part was planted with corn in 1943, and should yield results to air-photography, which should also reveal the course of the east side. The hill on which it lies is 700 ft. above the sea.

A furlong north of the north-west corner the Ythan, whose valley protects the north-west side, joins the Auld Davie—both tiny streams—and two roads join. Immediately north of this point, at the foot of Berry Hill of Achterless, now called Kirk Hill, the plans mark an earthwork, which the explanatory note on Roy's plate describes as 'the remains of an intrenchment having the same dimensions and proportions as the great camp; but the adjacent fields having been long under tillage, only fifty-seven yards of the whole work can now be seen'. This has now completely disappeared, though I thought I could see a slight difference in the growth of the corn. I do not, however, think it can have been Roman. Perhaps it was the traffic-rut of an old road.

Both plans mark three groups of pits in the region across the Ythan. I only inspected the site of those near the head of Auld Davie, but it is now a flat cornfield, revealing no signs of disturbance.

On the far north side of Kirk Hill the Ordnance map[2] marks a ditch one furlong long called 'Cumine's Trench'. (The name no doubt refers to the well-known Aberdeenshire family of that name, but need not have any original significance.) I was able to trace the ditch 500 ft. further at the bottom of the hill (the north-west end) and 1000 ft. on the top (south-east end), making a total length of nearly 2200 ft. The ditch has been levelled by cultivation, but it is still very wide and must originally have been deep. There seemed to be the remains of a bank on the south-west side, but of this

1 For once I find an apparent contradiction in Sir George's account. He states (p. 357) that the south (his south-west) rampart at the north extremity, where he and Professor Haverfield dug it, 'must originally have been about twenty feet thick', but lower down on the same page he gives the maximum width along this rampart as 11–12 ft.
2 Aberdeenshire, 27 N.E.

I could not be quite sure. The north-west end of the bank seems to continue across the stream in Owl's Den which also forms the boundary between the parishes of Auchterless and Forgue, and then to bend round southwards, but it disappears almost immediately. Before reaching the top of the hill it turns and runs due east for 200 ft., on the steepest part of the slope, then resumes its south-easterly direction. It continues over the rough ground on top of the hill, which has been ploughed at some time, and gradually falls into the line of a field-boundary which it joins at an obtuse angle; then it is lost. The line of this field-boundary, however, is continued, after a gap, by another which, after passing a spring, becomes a field-track leading to Logie Newton, on the Ythan, 700 yards north-east of the north-east corner of the Roman camp. The whole has the appearance of a defensive line covering the camp; but I am bound to admit that there is nothing in its design that looks at all characteristic of Roman work. It is considerably longer and further from the camp than the linear earthworks at Inchtuthil and Raedykes. Nevertheless, in view of the extreme rarity of such in Scotland, and the proximity of these three to known Roman sites, the possibility that it was made by the Romans should be borne in mind.

It remains only to mention the earthworks on the hill of Tillymorgan. There are two groups, on the north-west slopes and on the south-east. The plan in Roy marks two parallel lines almost completely encircling the hill. The explanatory note runs as follows: 'A little below the Mill of Cat-den[1] on the river Ury, two deep and large begin [sic], and becoming parallel near the Ferg road, proceed in that form all round the Mountain, for the space of two or three miles, till at last they disappear a little to north of the Kirk of Cul-sa-mon.' McRonald's plan shows them by firm lines between the Ury and the old Lawrence road and thence by lines of gradually diminishing strength. Moreover, McRonald shows the northern of the two as having a marked bend about the middle of its early course, which corresponds much more closely to the reality than the straight line of the engraved plate. I did not actually walk on the earthworks but looked at them from the Huntly road across the valley; from this view-point they did not seem to me to be either deep or large, but merely enclosure-banks of small dimensions and doubtful age; they are certainly not Roman and may perhaps be compared with the so-called 'circumvallations' round the hill of Burnswork in Dumfriesshire.

Of the many fragments of earthworks on the south-east slopes I could see

1 Spelt 'Caden' on McRonald's plan.

nothing though I walked over the ground. Cultivation has now completely obliterated them. Already when the explanatory note on the engraved plan was written, probably by Shand, the farmers had 'begun to carry off the earth of which the Rampart had been formed'. The chief earthwork is semi-circular, and where the northern segment meets Cadgers' road opposite the Mains of Tillymorgan (at N on the plan), 'there is', says the writer, 'a Ditch and Rampart of the same Length and Dimensions as the Traverses of the Re-dykes covering an opening of the works obliquely'. This sounded promising, but I could see no trace of anything in the grass field where it must have been situated. The site, at the foot of a steep hill, is a most unlikely one for a Roman camp, though there is a parallel at Burnswork.

We have now completed our survey of Glenmailen and its environs, and are free to resume our advance northwards; and there is now no Roman road to tempt us to loiter by the way. Covering 23 miles at one bound we alight at Bellie on the east bank of the Spey, 2½ miles above its mouth and 2 miles north of Fochabers. Here a Roman site is mentioned in Macfarlane's *Geographical Collections*[1] and by the writer of the *O.S.A.*[2] who gives it a tradi-tional name of 'Danish camp'. 'Large remains of the entrenchments' were then in existence, and 'from the square figure...it should rather seem to have been a Roman camp.' Chalmers marked it as a 'Roman camp' on his map of the district,[3] and published a description of it by 'the intelligent Colonel Imrie'. It was, to summarize the intelligent colonel's remarks, 'in form nearly a rectangular parallelogram of 888 feet by 333; but the west side, and the greatest part of the north end, are now wanting'. There was 'a small though perceptible deviation from the straight line' in the course of the east side. But he regarded it as his decided opinion that it was 'the work of a Roman army', the defences having 'nearly the same size as those of the camps of Battledykes in the county of Forfar'. Chalmers adds that the ford which it guards was the one used in April 1746 by the Duke of Cumber-land in his march to Culloden.

The camp is marked by a broken line on the Ordnance map[4] and the dimensions agree quite well with those of Colonel Imrie (south-west side 400 ft., south-east side 900 ft.). The south-east side, moreover, is marked as

---

1  I, 242: 1726.          2  XIV (1795), p. 271: parish of Bellie.          3  I, facing p. 129.
4  Elginshire (Moray), 9 s.w.  Robert Stuart (*Caledonia Romana*, 2nd ed. [1852], p. 219) records that 'some years since' the ditch was cleared out, but nothing was found 'except a few amulets or beads of party-coloured stone'. These do not sound like anything Roman.

curving outwards very slightly, though the curve is barely perceptible. The north-east side seems to be represented by a property boundary. The north-west side is formed by a steep cliff about 50 ft. high forming the eastern side of the Spey valley. The ground on which the camp lay is flat and undulating. At the north-west there is a gully or embayment in the cliff, probably caused by a spring, now enclosed in a cistern. In 1939 I had made arrangements to dig a few trial trenches to determine the character of the ditch, and I was allotted a grant for this purpose by the Society of Antiquaries of Scotland; but the war prevented the work being carried out. The war has also made future investigations much more difficult, for the camp-site has now reverted to its presumed original purpose (military hutments). I was there at an early enough date in the military occupation, however, to satisfy myself, by walking over the ground, with a roll of maps and an assumed air of confidence, that nothing whatever was now visible on the surface. The south-west side was being ploughed and may yet reveal the ditch by crop-marks. The south-east side, as marked on the map, crosses the road at an oblique angle and its north-eastern part passes along just inside the edge of the wood, but has left no traces there. We have therefore to rely on the plan, and on Colonel Imrie's description, in any attempt to form an opinion about its age. Against a Roman origin must be set the absence of any mention of defended entrances; surely an observer who was as familiar with Roman work as the Colonel was could not have failed to see and mention them if they were there. Then the size is against it, for it falls into none of the regular categories: it is too small for the smallest marching-camp of the kind we have hitherto met with in Scotland; but it does compare with the north marching-camp at Chew Green which is 982 × 625 ft., especially if we allow, as we well may, for a certain wastage due to the erosion of the cliff. I am not therefore inclined to rule it out on the ground of size. In favour of a Roman origin is the difficulty of assigning it to any other period. I know of no other medieval earthwork so long as this, and certainly it has no resemblance to any prehistoric or Dark Age fort. It is not big enough for a game-enclosure or a park. The site is also of exactly the kind so often selected by the Romans for forts and camps. If the Spey was to be crossed here there would quite certainly have been a fort to defend the crossing. On the analogy of Chew Green our camp should be the camp of the soldiers who were to build the fort, or to protect the builders; and there should be also here a labour-camp and a fort, if operations ever advanced so far. Air-photography may help here; meanwhile I regard the site as the most promising amongst all those mentioned whose true character remains doubtful. If authenticated it would bring the Roman penetration of Scotland to a point well north of any that has been suspected in modern times. It is therefore most desirable that the site should be excavated and air-photographed before it is too late to do so; and it may even now be too late.

[Since I wrote the above account, Mr R. F. Jessup has investigated the site from the air. He reports a 'rounded southern corner' seen very definitely in May 1943; and in September the crop-mark of a ditch which he is nearly certain links up with the corner previously seen. He also saw 'several large dark crop-marks, presumably pits, and what might have been a road travelling eastwards'. This tends to confirm a Roman origin, but there is still an element of uncertainty that only excavation can clear up. The attached plan (Fig. 32) is based on these observations.]

It would be wrong to conclude this survey without a brief mention of the important promontory-fort of Burghead on the coast of Moray between Lossiemouth and Forres, which has been claimed as Roman and wrongly identified with Ptolemy's Pteroton Stratopedon. I must plead guilty to having marked it as Roman myself, in a moment of temporary aberration, on a map which is fortunately little known and now out of print. It did not, however, escape the notice of Sir George Macdonald who quickly called me to order, referring me to his father's article in *P.S.A.S.* iv (1863), pp. 321–69, which gives a thorough survey of the discoveries made there. Up to then the only evidence produced for a Roman occupation was the well, which Dr James Macdonald compared with a similar well in the Broch of Burray, Orkney. It is still there and consists of a rock-hewn underground chamber, to which a modern arch and roofing of stone have been added. Dr Macdonald's attribution of the well to the broch-period may be correct; but no remains of any broch have been found here, and it may have been made by the builders of the Gallic fort, who certainly did make wells within their forts elsewhere. Since he wrote his account a coin of Nero has been found.[1] Certain 'bone-like buttons'[2] sound rather like Roman gaming-counters, but may be of another period. These discoveries are of course quite insufficient to prove Roman occupation; we may even go further and say that, if the very thorough ransacking which occurred in 1809 did not produce anything Roman, such negative evidence goes far to prove that (apart from the coin) Roman influence (much less the Romans themselves) can hardly have touched Burghead.

1 *P.S.A.S.* xxiv (1890), p. 146.        2 *P.S.A.S.* iv, 328.

The promontory was originally defended by multiple ramparts of dry stone walling bound together by a timber framework. Professor Childe has shown that this occurs also at Abernethy and Finavon and must be attributed to prehistoric Gallic invaders. A similar origin had already been suggested by

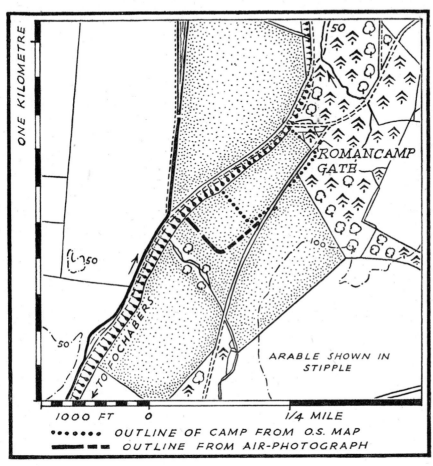

Fig. 32. Bellie, near Fochabers.

Mr H. W. Young[1] in 1891 for the Burghead work. To this period may belong the grain-pit in which a quantity of grain was found.[2] At a subsequent date there may have been a broch here.[3] During the Dark Ages the site was certainly occupied, as is shown by the remarkable stones sculptured with bulls, and by several fragments of carved crosses with animals and interlacing

1 *P.S.A.S.* xxv, 435–47.        2 P. 359.        3 P. 363.

work.[1] There is also a well called St Ethan's well near the shore almost half a mile east of the village, and I should be inclined to associate the name with Ethernan or Itharnan rather than with Aidan. This saint is said to have founded the church of Rathin in Buchan and to have died among the Picts in A.D. 669.[2] Occupation by the Vikings is securely attested by the discovery of the silver rim of a drinking-horn,[3] and to the same period no doubt belongs the coin of Alfred.[4] Less secure is the identification of Burghead with any of the places mentioned in the sagas; but Dr Macdonald thought it was the place there called Torfness and by Boece called Narmin. (One is tempted to associate Torfness with the promontory called Tarvedunon, 'bull-fort', by Ptolemy, on the strength of the sculptured bulls; but the position does not fit well. I cannot believe in the derivation from 'turf' which can never have been common enough at Burghead to give it a name, and is unlikely ever to have formed at all in such a place.) Occupation in medieval times[5] is proved by the presence of a chapel and graveyard (the latter still existing) where the cross and fragments were found, and by the discovery of a bronze jug.[6] In 1672 it was described as 'the town and sea-port of Burgsea'.[7] In 1809 the ramparts were ruthlessly levelled by the proprietor, an early profit-hunting capitalist, and the existing bleak unlovely slum was built.

Having thus brought you to the shores of the Moray Firth, you may well expect, like Agricola's long-suffering soldiers, to be allowed to return home in peace. Surely, you will say, the sea must be the limit? But have you forgotten those blue mountains across the firth? Our journey cannot end until we have examined every site where there seems, or has been thought to be, evidence that a Roman army might have camped; and the last such place is at Fortrose, a mile south-west of Rosemarkie. Here, in or just before 1853, two copper coins of Tiberius and Nero were found on the site of the bishop's palace.[8] Now I am not of course going to claim a Roman fort or camp on the evidence of two coins, which might well have been left there by the sailors of Agricola's naval reconnaissance of A.D. 84, or by later traders. But another origin is also possible. I have not visited the site, which was out of bounds when I was doing field-work in 1943; but on the map it looks a

1 P.S.A.S. IV, Plates XI and XII.　　2 Watson, Celtic Place-names, p. 321.
3 P.S.A.S. IV (1863), pp. 358, 377–8.　　4 P.S.A.S. X (1875), p. 586.
5 See also 'Burghead as the site of an early Christian church; with notices of the incised bulls and the burning of the clavie', by James Macdonald, Trans. Glasgow Arch. Soc. N.S. II (1896), pp. 63–115.
6 P.S.A.S. IV, 357.　　7 Ibid. p. 368.
8 P.S.A.S. I, 225–6; LII, 248.

likely one for a fort. The head of the Moray Firth is the logical Roman objective, short of which no attempt to subdue its southern shores could stop. If the site near Fochabers is ever proved to be Roman, the case for Fortrose will be strengthened. Till then it must remain no more than an attractive possibility.

After the above was written Mr Angus Graham informed me of a site visited by him and Professor Childe in September 1943. It is near the top of the low ridge that forms the spine of the Fort George promontory, and consists of an oval mound surrounded by a ditch and outer bank. Though more like a Roman signal-post than anything else, the oval shape is against it and the dimensions are rather too small.

## Chapter Eight

## THE HISTORICAL BACKGROUND

HAVING reached the end of our wanderings and seen all the known authentic Roman sites and some others, we are at last free to turn from topography to history. In dealing with this aspect of the Roman occupation I feel less at home than when going over ground that I know at first hand. My task has been rather to prepare the way for the historian than to emulate him. When so many competent hands have been at work, it is unlikely that much new information remains to be squeezed out of dry texts. I feel, moreover, a very special reluctance to compete, or even to appear to compete, with the leader we have just lost in what he had made his own special province. But this book would be incomplete without some sort of historical summary, however feeble, to set the facts in perspective and give them a coherent meaning. And here I wish to acknowledge the help that conversations with Professor Miller and Mr Ian Richmond have given to me in thinking out the historical sequence, with the proviso that they must not be held responsible for any opinions expressed.

We may dispose at once with the campaign of Severus, partly because virtually nothing is known of it, partly because none of the sites I have described can be associated with that emperor.[1] For the rest there is, with one exception, nothing but occasional brief references to North Britain in a few ancient writers, and nothing that throws light on the history of the area we have just traversed. That exception is the *Life of Agricola* by Tacitus which was written in A.D. 98 when its author was 43 years old. This biography has been praised for its literary charm, but it is not stated whether the charm lies in the 'rough, unpolished style' (*in candida ac rudi voce*) or in the extreme vagueness of the historical narrative. For, as has long been perceived, the main portion of the book is written as history rather than biography,[2] and as such it must be judged. Agricola's chief claim to fame lay in his conquest of Britain—or perhaps I should say, of part of Britain. The story of his life culminated in the seven campaigns. In describing the course of these campaigns Tacitus has achieved a record which must surely be unique, even

1 With the possible exception of the alleged Roman site, still unlocated, near Auchterderran, Fife, mentioned on p. 146.    2 Tacitus, *Agricola* (ed. Anderson), p. xxiii.

amongst literary men; he mentions only eleven geographical names in all.
Of these only seven are in the Scottish region, and five of them are rivers and
tribes. He mentions only two place-names proper (Mons Graupius, Portus
Trucculensis) without giving the slightest clue to their position. Imagine
a modern Italian biography of Graziani which mentioned only Massawa
and Macallé! Even an occasional mention of distance or day's march would
have been helpful, but there is none. We are not told the name of any of
Agricola's headquarters, nor even in what parts of the island they were situated.
Dr Johnson, no mean judge in these matters, had a low opinion of Tacitus,
who seemed to him 'rather to have made notes for an historical work, than
to have written a history'.[1]

But we must, I suppose, be grateful for the miserable fare provided; and
indeed the task of extracting history from it has a certain rather irritating
attraction, akin to cross-word problems. It is a game that has been played
for over two centuries, and is still going on. There is no reason to suppose
that my own efforts, of which I am slightly ashamed, will be any more
successful than many others.

The first two years of Agricola's governorship were concerned with Wales
and North Britain. The third year (A.D. 80)[2] 'opened up new tribes, the
natives being harried as far as the estuary of the Tay'. The reading usually
adopted for the estuary-name is Tanaum, but the old and good *Codex Aesinas*
has a variant reading Taum. There is no river Tanaus and I felt convinced
that the Tay must have been intended, though Anderson[3] thought that
'Agricola cannot possibly have got so far thus early in his campaign'.
I consulted Mr Richmond (who has dealt with this and many other problems far more effectively than I can, in a paper on Agricola which has been
published in the *Journal of Roman Studies*);[4] and I am glad that he sees no
reason why the Tay should not have been reached in A.D. 80. 'This', he
says, 'was a reconnaissance campaign, followed by temporary concentration
on the Forth-Clyde line. You usually go further than the line you select for
concentration, and the Tay seems to me logical enough.'[5]

The fourth year (A.D. 81) was devoted to consolidating the conquests of

1 Boswell's *Life of Johnson*, I, ed. Roger Ingpen (1907), p. 414.
2 There is an uncertainty about the actual dates, which may be one year earlier. I have
adopted the later dating, which seems best supported. The point is not of any real importance
here, and is fully discussed by Anderson (*Cornelii Taciti de Vita Agricolae*, Oxford [1922],
pp. 166–73).   3 P. 106.
4 *Journ. Roman Studies*, XXXIV, 1944, pp. 34–45.   5 Letter of 16 August 1943.

the previous year, chiefly in the lowlands, by building forts along the line which 60 years later was to become the Antonine Wall.

The fifth year (A.D. 82) was spent in 'subduing hitherto unknown tribes', presumably in the south-west of Scotland; for he also 'manned with troops that part of Britain which faces Ireland'. Here is a region where we may well hope for startling discoveries.

In the sixth year (A.D. 83) he 'embraced in his operations the tribes beyond the Forth and explored the harbours with his fleet', which kept close contact with the land forces. The army was divided into three divisions and there was a night battle in one of the camps.

The invasion of Scotland culminated, during the seventh and last campaign (A.D. 84), in the famous battle of Mons Graupius. Of the site, all that we know for certain, thanks to Sir George Macdonald, is that it lay some distance north of Inchtuthil,[1] which one may regard as Agricola's advanced base and subsequent winter quarters. No one, so far as I know, has suggested that Agricola invaded the Highlands; and his contact with the fleet soon after the battle implies that he was not far from the sea. He can only have followed the time-honoured route along Strathmore, where we find that series of marching-camps which Melville, arguing from similar premises, so brilliantly forecast and discovered. The narrative of Tacitus implies that Mons Graupius was at some distance from Agricola's starting-point (which we may take to have been Inchtuthil), and also that there was a marching-camp there. It can hardly have been less than 25 miles beyond and was probably much further; so that, of the known marching-camps, we have to choose between Keithock, perhaps Fordoun, Raedykes, Normandykes, perhaps Kintore, and Glenmailen. Keithock may be ruled out at once as too small.

When we were discussing the problem together, Professor Miller pointed out to me that the site of the battle must have been at some place which Calgacus knew the Romans must pass in their advance northwards. Before Agricola set out, Calgacus had collected his forces there, and Agricola knew it (*montem Graupium . . . quem jam hostis insederat*). Now there are at least two possible routes along Strathmore—along the foothills of the Grampians on the north-west side or along the lower slopes of the Sidlaws on the high ground in the south-east. Both routes converge towards Stonehaven where the mountains reach the sea, and an advancing army is there confined to a corridor of less than 4 miles in width. Here is the bottle-neck,

1 *J.R.S.* IX, 115.

and here only are there no alternative routes. But once this corridor is passed there are again many possible lines of advance. Precisely here at this bottle-neck is the camp of Raedykes.

Let us now examine Tacitus' account of the site of the battle. One gets an impression of an open place (*veniunt e latebris suis extrusi...in aperto*) reached after a long march through marshes, rivers and woods (*paludes montesve et flumina*, ch. 33; *silvas saltusque penetrantibus;* [*hostes*] *quos tandem invenistis*, ch. 34). The battle was begun on a plain between the Roman camp on the one side and hills on the other, with woods not far off (*Britannorum acies...editioribus locis constiterat, media campi covinnarius eques strepitu ac discursu complebat*, ch. 35; *erigere in colles aciem coepere*, ch. 36; *Britanni...summa collium insederant, postquam silvas appropinquaverunt*, ch. 37). There was at least one native village within sight of the Roman camp, probably on a hill (*deserere domos ac per iram incendere; deserti colles, fumantia procul tecta*, ch. 38). Tacitus, moreover, nowhere mentions a river, and if there was one such on the battlefield, it would have had such tactical importance that it must surely have been mentioned. If this last omission correctly represents the facts, we can rule out Normandykes on the Dee decisively, and the possible camps at Fordoun and Kintore with nearly equal confidence. There remain only Raedykes and Glenmailen. But the topography of Glenmailen is such that, as Haverfield pointed out, 'no battle in the least resembling that sketched by Tacitus could have been fought here with the Roman fort resting on the river', and it can only be identified with Mons Graupius 'on the assumption that the Romans that day faced south, and that the Ythan guarded their rear',[1] which seems to me most unlikely. Even so, Glenmailen, though in high and open country, has no small hills near it on the south.

Raedykes satisfies all these requirements (Fig. 28). It faces north along a gently rising but fairly level ridge, beyond which are the hills of Curlethney, Meikle Carewe and (on the west) Campstone. On the last hill is a native village represented by a group of some twenty or more hut-circles, plainly visible from the Roman camp at a distance of less than half a mile. It is, and must always have been, an open treeless upland, surrounded by tree-covered lower ground and thickly wooded valleys. This upland is the extreme eastern spur of the granite mountains that extend westwards to the Atlantic. On the east, on lower ground, are the great peat-bogs of Megray and the Red Moss and many others. Between these dangerous swamps and wooded valleys on

1 *J.R.S.* ix, 359, quoting 'Roman Britain in 1913', *British Academy Supplementary Papers*, ii, pp. 8 ff.

the east, north and south, and the difficult mountains on the west, the ridge
of Raedykes leads like an open corridor to northern Scotland. It was the
obvious way from Strathmore to Aberdeenshire in early days, from Southern
to Northern Pictland in the Dark Ages. Here the invader must pass and
here he must be stopped before he escapes into the vast open spaces beyond,
where he can manœuvre and retain his initiative.

There is even more suggestive evidence of a battle here. Remains of no
less than three wheels have been found at Raedykes, one being actually
found on the bottom of the ditch of the north side itself.[1] Between 1822 and
1845 a complete wheel was dug up within the camp, and fragments are still
preserved in Fetteresso Castle; and before 1822 'a small hoop or ring of iron',
explained as an axle-ring, was found, also in the ditch. Surely these can
only be the remains of the war-chariots which Tacitus describes manœuvring
over the plain just in front of the camp? Wheels have been found in the
Roman forts of Bar Hill and Newstead; the one at Bar Hill was perfect and
little worn, and Sir George gives reasons for thinking it may have belonged,
not to a Roman cart, but to a native vehicle 'of more than usual importance',
perhaps 'the relic of an assault repelled'.[2] One cannot help feeling, in the
face of these revelations, that had not his habitual native caution restrained
him, Sir George himself might have entered the lists as a supporter of the
Mons Graupius identification of Raedykes. He did not do so, however, and
confined himself to the statement that it was 'by no means impossible that
the three wheels...may have belonged to the Roman period'[3]—surely an
understatement since one fragment was found by himself in the bottom of
the ditch and therefore presumably, by all the rules of excavation, contemporary with or older than the camp?

But if Raedykes is Mons Graupius, to whom should we attribute the
construction of the two, or three, Roman camps north of it? If we can trust
Tacitus, and I am quite willing not to, Agricola after the battle led his army
back, or down (*deducit*) into the territory of the Boresti, from whom he took
hostages; he then told the commander of his fleet to sail round (*circumvehi*)
Britain, and marched back slowly to his winter quarters. It goes without
saying that Tacitus gives no hint as to the location of the Boresti; nor are
they mentioned by any other writer. To account for this rather curious
sequence of events Tacitus calls in the weather; it was too late in the year
for the war to be 'spread' (*exacta jam aestate spargi bellum nequibat*, ch. 38).
The narrative is, as usual, obscure; and whether it means that, after the

1 *P.S.A.S.* L, 343.          2 *P.S.A.S.* XL, 499.          3 *P.S.A.S.* L, 344.

battle, Agricola advanced further or retreated depends upon the exact meaning of *deducit* which I am not competent to assess. It is certainly not necessary to infer an advance, for from Raedykes one would be described as leading an army downwards, whether one led it northwards to the Dee or south-eastwards to the coast, and the same is true of Glenmailen. No doubt Agricola intended to consolidate Strathmore before undertaking his next campaign; and it was with the next season in view that he sent his fleet on their reconnaissance voyage, to find out how much further north the land extended. Although he himself might have been prevented, by his recall, from carrying the Roman arms beyond the Dee, we now know that he or one of his successors did build at least one fort (and probably more) in the territory won during his last campaign; and in any case it must have been he or one of his successors who, unknown and unsung, carried the advance beyond the Grampians and made the marching-camps of Normandykes and Glenmailen. We know a good deal about Agricola because his daughter married a writer; but there may have been other generals just as good or better of whom no account was written.

In any case I cannot believe that the Romans stopped at Glenmailen. They must surely have reached the Moray Firth which is the logical objective when once the area north of the Grampians has been entered. Air-photography and excavation alone can decide.

# Appendix 1

## NOTE ON FINDS NEAR FENDOCH

IMMEDIATELY north of the farm of Fendoch[1] the Ordnance map (Perthshire, 84 s.w.) has the following entry: 'Urns, camp-kettles, broken spears, and pieces of armour found A.D. 1834.' No exact spot is marked, but the site indicated is on the high ground south of the Perth road and south-east of the 'redoubt'. I am once more indebted to Mr Thomas McLaren for unearthing and sending me a contemporary record of this discovery, published in the *Perthshire Courier*, 4 September 1834, which runs as follows:

'**Logie-almond: relics of antiquity.** As some men were lately digging in an enclosure belonging to Mr Moray of Abercairney, on the site of the Roman camp in Glenalmond, they came upon a very large pot which broke into pieces on being handled. With it were found two smaller vessels, in the form of goblets with a long handle attached to each. With these were lying three spear ends, three branks of a very strong make, two pairs of irons, a pair of hinges mounted with silver, and two parcels of buckles tied together.'

The *N.S.A.* (Vol. x, *Perth* [1845], p. 274) gives an independent but in some respects more detailed account, here summarized. The name of the finder is given as Donald Stewart, the date August (instead of September) 1834. He was 'digging across the eastern rampart of the camp, for the purpose of constructing a stone fence': clearly the camp referred to was the large alleged marching-camp. The 'very large pot' and 'two smaller vessels' of the *Courier* account are lumped together as 'three pots or kettles'. The two which were unbroken are described as 'composed of a series of concentric circles, fastened together with nails, and the larger pot, having a straight handle 21 inches in length', was 10 in. in diameter and $4\frac{1}{2}$ in. in depth. (The smaller was $8\frac{1}{2} \times 3$ in.) The 'branks' of the earlier account are called 'three pair of bits'; the 'irons' appear to correspond to 'shears'; the 'pair of hinges' is described as 'a beautiful hinge of a yellowish metal, still covered with a slight coating of what appears to be silver, 4 inches in length, carved, and in excellent preservation'. The later account omits any mention of the 'buckles', but otherwise agrees fairly well with the older; it also mentions the following objects not mentioned there:

1. A piece of flat iron or other metal, $18\frac{1}{2}$ inches in length, having a striking resemblance to a Roman sword preserved in the Museum of Antiquities, Edinburgh, except that the latter measures 25 inches in length. [But the one from Fendoch was broken.]
2. A sort of spoon, the handle of which measures 10 inches, including the diameter of the mouth. [It is compared to a 'thuribulum found in Pompeii'.]

---

[1] The farm has no name on the Ordnance map; it is the long building 1100 ft. east of the fourteenth milestone from Perth. It is called Middle Fendoch on the map of 1778 (Plate VI).

3.  Two implements resembling the wimble used by carpenters for boring.
4.  A piece of flat iron about 2½ feet long, bent in the form of a pair of sugar-tongs.
5.  Other articles whose uses were not very apparent.

The account adds that 'the whole of the articles above described, except the hinge and one of the spears, have found a secure asylum in the custody of John Buchanan, Esq., Secretary to the Western Bank, Glasgow, whose property they have become'.  But the alleged 'security' was illusory; when Dr Christison tried, in or before 1898, to trace the objects, through the heirs of Mr Buchanan, he failed to do so.

Two possible strays from this hoard may be mentioned.  One is the bronze ladle and strainer in the National Museum.[1]  It is tempting to identify this with the long-handled goblets of the original record, but the measurements of these given in the *N.S.A.* do not agree with those of the specimens now at Edinburgh.  Moreover, the ladle and strainer is said to have been found in Glenshee, the name of the head of the Shochie Burn, 5½ miles north-east of Fendoch, in the parish of Logie-almond.

A more likely stray is a brass lamp said to have been found at Fendoch which was bought from an old lady who had charge of the post office at Buchanty, less than a mile east of the site where the hoard was found.  It was sold by auction at Christmas, 1942, by the widow of a Perth solicitor.  It was about 3 in. high and 3½ in. broad, with four lips for wicks, and it stood on three legs.  (I am indebted to Mr Thomas McLaren for this information, conveyed to me in his letter of 28 May 1943.)

No definite conclusions can be drawn from these facts.  The ladle and strainer is assigned 'probably' to the second century A.D. by Mr James Curle; but as we have seen there are difficulties in accepting it as part of the hoard.  Perhaps this description may be read by someone who can throw further light on the matter, or knows what became of the objects.  Are they possibly still in the vaults of the Glasgow bank?

1  *P.S.A.S.* XXI (1887), p. 263; LXVI (1932), p. 386, fig. 16 on p. 306.

# Appendix 2

## THE GASK SIGNAL-POSTS TABULATED

| No. (Crawford) | NAME Dr Christison's no. in brackets *P.S.A.S.* XXV | DISTANCES (in feet) | DIAMETER OF PLATFORM (in feet) | O.S.* 6 in. map (Perthshire) | Excavated 1900 | External bank | Rema |
|---|---|---|---|---|---|---|---|
| 1 | Parkneuk (1) | 6380† | — | 107 N.W. | — | — | — |
| 2 | Raith | 5000 | — | (107 N.W.) | — | — | — |
| 3 | Ardunie | 5000 | 39 | (107 N.W.) | — | — | — |
| 4 | Kirkhill (2) | 6780 | 46‡ | (108 N.E.) | Yes | Yes | — |
| 5 | Muir o' Fauld (3) | 4700 | 52 | (108 N.E.) | Yes | — | — |
| 6 | Gask (4) | 2900 | 45§ | 108 N.E. | Yes | — | — |
| 7 | Witch Knowe (5) | 2660 | 44‡ | 108 N.E. | Yes | Yes | Plan publis |
| 8 | Moss-side (6) | 3620 | 51 (mound) | 97 S.W. | Yes | — | Plan publis |
| 9 | Midgate (7) | 4400 | 42 (measured from middle of ditch) | 97 S.W. | Yes | — | Plan publis (the ( site is wrong |

* Brackets indicate that it is not marked on the current edition.
† From Strageath.
‡ Christison's measurements.
§ Christison gives 35 ft.

# Appendix 3

## OTHER REMAINS EAST AND SOUTH OF FORFAR

**Alleged Roman road, Oathlaw to Kirkbuddo.** Mr Jameson, in Gough's *Camden*, IV (1806), p. 153, gives an elaborate description of what he calls a 'military way' from the marching-camp at Oathlaw to that at Kirkbuddo. It was composed of 'rough, unpolished stones (commonly called bullet-stones) and earth', and pursued a devious course with sharp turns. It passed an old cottage called Stonypaths, crossed some ramparts running east and west along the slopes of the hill of Carse, then went by the farm of Broom-Knows on the estate of Carsebank, crossed the Brechin-Forfar road near the 'Picts' Camp', where it crossed another ditch and rampart, and could be traced for nearly a mile over a moor.

This is plainly no Roman road; but the remains described no doubt did exist and were perhaps prehistoric. I spent a whole day looking for traces of its continuation southwards nearer the camp of Kirkbuddo, where Maitland[1] mentions the recent discovery of a 'military way' on the western side of the camp, leading to the 'fortress'. But my investigations were not guided as closely as they should have been by these descriptions and the accompanying map—one cannot carry folio volumes about the country on a bicycle, and they are not to be found in provincial towns. I should like to go over the ground again; but, while there may be discoveries to be made, I doubt whether they will prove to be Roman.

**Picts' Camp and Ditch, Lunanhead.** The 'Picts' Camp' just mentioned still exists at Lunanhead, on the north-west side of the Brechin road immediately north of the railway bridge. It seems, together with the many cist-burials found round it, and the standing-stones to the east, to have been responsible for Buchanan's invention of the Battle of Restennet, A.D. 830, between Feredith and Alpin. Since then, by inverted reasoning, it has been cited as evidence for the fictitious battle! Macfarlane[2] refers only to the battle. Melville, in 1754, made a sketch-plan of it, under the name of Cloghton;[3] and it is marked on Jameson's plan of the alleged Roman road just described.[4] The Ordnance Survey *Object Name-book* (*c.* 1860)[5] describes the fosse as 'pretty entire except on the west'. The accompanying 6 in. map marks its outline, but this was removed on the later editions. But the rampart and ditch were still plainly visible (as marked) when I saw it in 1939, except on the east and west sides. The overall width of the south side was 30 yards. It was then under grass, but when I passed it in 1943 it was under plough and an excellent subject for air-photography.

1 *History* (1757), p. 200.    2 I (1743), p. 278.

3 *P.S.A.S.* LXXIII (1939), pp. 247–8.

4 Gough's *Camden*, IV (1806), facing p. 153.    5 Pp. 9, 10.

It has been described as a rectangle with rounded corners, but I cannot see it as such, and should describe it rather as an oval whose longer diameter, east-north-east to west-south-west, is about 660 ft. and shorter about 500 ft., so that it is probably native.

Prehistoric cist-burials have frequently been found at Lunanhead, the finds including jet beads and a beaker.[1] Jet beads, indeed, seem to have been common here in the Bronze Age, for a fine necklace found (with another?) in a cist 100 yards north-east of Pitreuchie Farm is preserved there, with the stones of the cist, by Mrs Graham, who showed them to me in 1939.[2]

Jameson also mentions a 'ditch and rampart' which his map marks and says they were 'drawn by the Picts between the Lochs of Forfar and Resteneth to guard their camp'. In 1939 I noted on the map what I described as an 'old wall or bank' running from a large oval mound, perhaps natural, at Lunan Well, parallel to the railway, crossing the Brechin road immediately south of the railway bridge. The portion observed is over a quarter of a mile long, but I did not follow it westwards, as at the time I did not connect it with the ditch and rampart marked by Jameson, which it seems to represent. A native linear earthwork utilizing lakes has been described near Melrose;[3] this is also a characteristic feature of the Black Pig's Dyke in Ireland.

**Alleged Roman camp, Guynd.** The *N.S.A.*[4] mentions vestiges of an encampment called Dunhead on a hill between two ravines called the Black Den and the Den of Guynd, in Carmylie parish. It was described as of triangular form, precipitous on two sides, and defended on the other by a ditch and rough wall or dyke. This is the 'entrenchment on Down Head Hill near Arbirlot' of which Melville made a rough sketch-plan in July 1754. It is described as 'Roman camp' on the Ordnance map,[5] and a bank is marked. For the greater part of its course (on the east and south) this bank is low, has no ditch and has large trees (beeches) growing on it—a feature always suggestive of former field-boundaries. The north-east part of the little plateau has been under cultivation, as proved by the presence of rigs and furrows. The bank is therefore probably (like that at Drumsleed, p. 107) the boundary of cultivation. The most easterly point of the bank is bigger than the rest, and has a ditch, but it is on the wrong (east) side. Stone cists were found close-by on the north; but apart from these there seems to be no evidence of ancient occupation of the site.

**Alleged Roman camp, Catter Milley.** Maitland (I, 215) describes a 'Roman camp about 200 yards square' 2 miles west of Dundee, 'fortified with a high rampart and spacious ditch', the south side 'fenced with triple ramparts and ditches....The

1 *P.S.A.S.* II (1859), p. 190; XII (1878), p. 288; LXXVI (1942), p. 128; *Arch. Scot.* II (1842), p. 91.
2 At the same time I was shown, and inserted on the map, the site of St Boniface's chapel, 500 ft. north-north-east of Blindwell (Macfarlane, *Geogr. Collections*, I [1743], p. 272; *Arch. Scot.* II [1822], p. 23). This is on the site of Feradeth or Feridan field, the alleged site of the battle of A.D. 830.
3 *Antiquity*, X (1936), pp. 346–9.          4 *Forfarshire* (1845), p. 358.
5 Forfarshire, 45 S.E.

other sides being demolished by the plow, the vestigia appear but faintly'; but they were sufficient to show that this fortress was of a parallelogram form, about a quarter of a mile in length. Maitland's account was copied by all subsequent writers who add nothing except the tale of gradual obliteration. It had already gone in 1831 when Knox wrote; but his account does enable us to fix the site, for he describes it as immediately south of the former lake of Lochee, and marks it there on his map. We are thus able to identify it with the 'supposed site of Castle' of the Ordnance map (Forfarshire, 53 N.E.). This consists of a rectangular area 200 × 100 ft., the larger axis north and south, with projections at each corner. There is no description of it in the old *Object Name-books*. I have walked all over the site, which was under grass at the time, and can make nothing of it. There are a lot of stones at the site of the 'castle', and there may have been some building there. Maitland's description is ambiguous and inconsistent, for if it was '200 yards square' it cannot also have had a 'parallelogram form, about a quarter of a mile in length'. The triple ramparts also sound suspicious. If it is now again under plough, it should be air-photographed.

# Appendix 4

## ADDITIONAL SITES (MOSTLY NON-ROMAN)

IT seems unnecessary to catalogue all references to earthworks for which a Roman origin has been claimed, for many of them may be dismissed at sight as 'native' or medieval. One should remember that not until some years after the *New Statistical Account* appeared was there any large-scale Ordnance map to elucidate the topography and plan of such sites; and that with its aid one can often eliminate them without even visiting the spot. I have not been able to visit all the sites in the following list, but for the benefit of future investigators I have tabulated the chief facts about them.

### ABERDEENSHIRE

**Auchingoul** (18 N.W.). Chalmers was informed by Shand of 'the obvious remains of military works' here. But a note in the *O.S.A.* shows that Shand was trying to find a route for the spurious itinerary of Richard of Cirencester. In doing so he was influenced by an alleged Roman site at Deskford, which as we shall see is probably non-Roman. I much doubt whether Shand was really convinced of the Roman nature of the site at Auchingoul; his words seem intentionally non-committal. The remains are marked on the Ordnance map. They are on a tongue of land between a small rivulet and the Deveron, at a point 1½ miles north-west of Inverkeithing and close to the Mains of Auchingoul. They consist of a maze of irregularities that suggest modern digging on an ancient site. On the opposite side of the Deveron (the left or north-east bank) is marked 'Wallace's camp', but no earthworks are shown, merely the natural bank of the river. I have not visited the site, but have no great hopes of it as a Roman one.

    *O.S.A.* xii (1794), p. 315 (note).
    Chalmers, i (1807), p. 127.
    *Arch. Scotica*, iv (1857), App. p. 29.

**Causewayend, Huntly** (26 N.E.). The *N.S.A.* claims a Roman road here, coming from Sliach through Knightland moss. This road is merely the Huntly end or branch of the medieval road already discussed (p. 115).

    *N.S.A.* xii (1845), p. 302.

**Robin's Height, Drumblane** (26 S.E.). This is marked 'Camp (site of), A.D. 1307' on the map, and it is claimed as Roman by the *N.S.A.* The Ordnance description suggests that it was regarded as the camping-site of an army before a battle. There is no sign of irregularity on the top of this smooth rounded eminence as seen from the road, but I did not walk over it. Probably a native fort gave rise to both these claims. It is now wholly under cultivation and is a good site for an air-photograph.

    *N.S.A.* xii (1845), p. 301.

**Forgue** (27 s.w.). The Ordnance map (edition of 1873) marks 'supposed site of Roman road' against the track leading south-eastwards from the cross-roads south-west of Blackhills ('old sand-pit') to the modern road between Bridge of Dyce on the north to Crofts of Heathfield on the south. This is called the road 'to Huntly' on McRonald's map of 1789 (see Plate XX). It is now a field-track with a deep traffic-rut beside it representing the medieval road. The 'Roman' attribution was rightly omitted on the second (1901) edition of the map.

O.S. *Object Name-book*, parish of Forgue, p. 97.

**Seed Hill, Forgue.** This is marked on the plan of Glenmailen in Roy and on McRonald's map. The explanatory note on Roy's plate (probably written by Shand) describes it as 'a ring-post near the summit of the Seed-hill of Achaber, with a ditch and rampart well preserved and distinct; the diameter of the whole work is 48 feet, and the interior part half that extent'. From the dimensions given this sounds more like a signal-post of the Gask type than anything else (compare p. 136); but it is more likely to have been some kind of native work. It stood on high ground and a Roman road is said to have passed from it to Forgue, Rothiemay and the Spey; but this is probably a confused reference to the medieval road three-quarters of a mile to the south-west. The *N.S.A.* gives the diameter as 60 ft.; perhaps this was the overall diameter. The Ordnance map of 1873 marked the 'site of camp' at a point on the south-east edge of Seed Hill Plantation 400 ft. north-east of the south corner of the wood; this was omitted from the second edition of 1901. The *Object Name-book* records that no traces were visible at the time of the original survey.

Roy, Plate LI.
*N.S.A.* XII (1845), p. 601.
*Object Name-book*, parish of Forgue, p. 86.

**Bethelnie, Old Meldrum** (36 s.e.). About 1150 ft. west by south of the farm of Bethelnie the map marks 'Earthwork (site of)' by a rectangular enclosure of broken lines about 260 ft. square. It lies in a cornfield near the foot of a hill on the north but on level ground. The ditch on the south side can still be seen both from the road to the north and on the site; but the ditch on the north can only be seen, and that indistinctly, from a distance. There are practically no remains of any banks visible. There are no signs of entrances and no evidence that it is Roman, and it is more likely to be a medieval moated site. An air-photograph would decide.

On the other hand it was regarded as Roman by Shand, and it seems possible (though the point is of minor importance only) that it was this site rather than that on Barra Hill[1] nearby which was described by Newte (probably in words composed by Shand) as a 'very remarkable presidium'. Shand's opinion is given in the original paper he wrote for the Perth Society in or about 1788, which was long missing but has now turned up amongst the archives of that Society preserved in the Perth Library

---

[1] Shand also regarded this fine prehistoric fort as Roman.

and Museum.[1] His words are: 'The work at the south-west foot of the hill of Bethelnie in the parish of Fyvie, and three miles north-west of Old Meldrum, has every appearance of being a military one. It is also a square, of almost sixty to seventy paces to a side, very entire, and the ditch and rampart of the dimensions usually given to the temporary camps of the Romans.' It will be observed that there is no reference to entrances or corners. Shand also regarded Fortingall, a certainly medieval earthwork, not unlike this though smaller (see p. 78), as Roman; he was a good and careful observer, but not infallible.

> *Observations on Roman Camps*, by Captain Shand: Perth Library.
> *N.S.A.* XII (1845), p. 477.
> *P.S.A.S.* L (1916), p. 350, quoting—
> Thomas Newte, *A Tour in England and Scotland* (1791), p. 301.

**King's Howe and Ford, Fyvie and Daviot** (36 S.E.). Macfarlane records this as the site of one of Bruce's camps. The Ordnance Survey *Object Name-book* quotes from *Collections* (probably those of Macfarlane) to the same effect, and adds that it was a native camp, and that the ditches were still very entire, 'and are about 12 inches [*sic*] in depth, and the artificial banks are still visible'. If this is a description of the remains marked by hachures in Kingshill Wood and called 'earthworks' it is certainly incorrect. These are simply the traffic-ruts of an old road; there are others, not marked, parallel to the existing road, in the north-west part of the wood. Both groups converge on the ford over the King's Burn, a small stream, and the easternmost rut of the eastern group is still in use as a cart-track. They seem to enclose the higher ground— a fact which has no doubt led to their being regarded as the defences of a native fort by Captain Courtney and the earlier writers. The hill on the north-east side of the burn is called King's Howe. Though not claimed as Roman the site is included here as it was visited and its precise nature determined. The 'Cloven stone' south-west of it is a large rock split into two parts along a line running north and south. There are many smaller stones round it, possibly remains of a cairn; but the whole may be of natural origin.

> Macfarlane, I (1724), p. 84.
> *Object Name-book*, parish of Daviot (1867), p. 13, quoting—
> *Collections of the Shires of Aberdeen and Banff*, p. 580.

**Pitcaple, Chapel of Garioch** (45 s.w.). This site was claimed as a 'Roman outpost' by Shand; but in a footnote he states, without comment, that in the opinion of 'some of the well-informed neighbours' he was wrong in his attribution, 'it being only the remains of a castle belonging to the Leslies'. Captain Courtney examined the site very carefully and came to the conclusion that it was 'only a small affair', corresponding very nearly in dimensions with what he, following others, regarded as the 'Roman post at Fortingal, in Glen Lyon'. At the time of his survey (1867) the

---

1 I am indebted to their custodian, Mr McLaren, for showing me this paper, which Sir George Macdonald failed to locate there (under another regime).

site was under cultivation and part of the earthwork had already been 'removed' by the father of the then tenant. The remains lie on flat ground on the edge of the steep north side of the river Urie, immediately above a sharp bend in it, a quarter of a mile north-west of Pitcaple Castle. The site was under grass when I walked over it in May 1943. It appears to be triangular. The ramparts are just visible, that on the north being about 300 ft. long, and appearing to have been dug into in two places; it runs east and west. The south-east rampart, if such it is, runs south-westwards, forming an angle of about 45° with the north rampart; but it is now of the nature of a scarp rather than a rampart proper. The west side, which is at right angles to the north, is shorter and less plainly visible. There is clearly nothing Roman here. Nearby were found the foundations of a bridge, and on the original 6 in. map a 'Roman' road (omitted from the 1901 edition) was marked, leaving the earthwork at the south-west end of the south-east rampart and running south-eastwards across river, road and railway for nearly half a mile; but it is not straight, nor, I think, Roman.

O.S.A. xii (1794), p. 313 (mention only, without description).
P.S.A.S. vii (1869), pp. 28–9 (Shand, 1798).
N.S.A. xii (1845), pp. 570, 734.
Object Name-book, Chapel of Garioch (13), p. 34 (earthwork, Courtney, 1867).
Ibid. p. 35 (road, Courtney, 1867).
P.S.A.S. vii (1869), p. 388 (Courtney).

## ANGUS

**Clatto Moor, Strathmartin** (49 s.e.). On the top of a hill between Clatto Reservoir and Rosemill the Ordnance map marks the site of a camp 'supposed Roman'. The O.S.A. records a 'tradition' that Wallace pitched his camp on Clatto Hill. There were traces only in 1794. I have not visited the site, but it is probably that of a native fort.

O.S.A. xiii (1794), p. 99.
N.S.A. Forfarshire (1845), p. 57 ('some vestiges').

## BANFFSHIRE

**Deskford** (9 n.w.). The O.S.A. definitely states that Roman coins were found here, and Chalmers adds that they were found 'some years ago, near the old bridge, a little below the Tower of Deskford. The coins were given to the Earl of Findlater, the lord of the manor.' He then goes on to quote Gordon's description of a small hoard of twenty-seven or more Roman coins preserved by the Earl of Findlater. Sir George Macdonald identifies this hoard with the coins found at Deskford 'some years' before 1807. Gordon wrote in 1726, and 'some years' seems a curious expression for 80 years or more. But the two finds may be identical for all that. In any case it seems certain that Roman coins *were* found at Deskford.

The Rev. Mr Lawtie, minister of Fordyce, claimed to have found at Deskford 'a Roman station, which he conceived to have the form of an oblong square, along the west side of the rivulet Culen; comprehending ten acres, with the Tower, the church, and manse, and the village of Deskford'. Chalmers got Mr George Brown, the professional surveyor who had made a plan of Raedykes in 1785 (*P.S.A.S.* L [1916], pp. 328–31), to survey the remains in November 1799. 'To his more accurate eyes, the entrenchments appeared so indistinct, that it was impossible to determine, by what people, or for what purpose, they had been made.'

Besides the alleged 'station' there was a length of 'about 450 yards of an old paved road, leading from the south-east directly up to this supposed station'. Mr Lawtie thought it Roman, but 'the indifferent eyes of Mr Brown saw nothing but a regular causeway over a deep clay soil, which necessity may have caused to be made here in much more recent times'. Colonel Shand saw the road in the summer of 1801 and informed Chalmers that it was 'evidently very old, and is certainly paved, like the Roman roads, but is much broken at the sides; and it does not proceed in a straight line, like the Roman roads, in Strathern'.

All this is very dubious; but there were Roman coins found here, and the site therefore should be watched.

Gordon, *Itin. Sept.* 1726, p. 186 (this or another site?).
*O.S.A.* IV (1792), p. 358; XII (1794), p. 315 (road, Shand).
Chalmers, I (1807), p. 128, n. i; quoted above.
*Object Name-book*, parish of Deskford, p. 12.

## FIFE

**Newport** (1 S.W., formerly 2 N.E.). The 'site of a Roman camp (supposed)' was marked on the 1855 edition of the 6 in. Ordnance map (2 N.E.) on the quite valueless evidence of local opinion; and the name was rightly removed in 1894. The 'camp' was destroyed about 1835 and consisted of a round earthen bank with a cairn in the centre, in the middle of which was found a coffin, made of 'roughly polished yellow sandstone' [*sic*]. One of the slabs, which in 1866 stood near Tayfield House, was about 6 ft. long, 4 ft. broad, and 6 in. thick. Anything less like a Roman camp it is difficult to imagine!

*P.S.A.S.* VI (1867), p. 392.
*Object Name-book* (1854), parish of Forgan, p. 76.
Ibid. (1894), Fife, 1 S.W. (10, 14), p. 13.
Christison, *Early Fortifications*, p. 68.

**Lochore, Ballingry** (26 S.E.). Gordon describes this site as follows: '...Lochore about two miles from Loch Leven in Fyffe, and a Quarter of a Mile from the House of Sir John Malcolm, on whose ground it stands, and is situated near a Lake called Lochore: The Form of this Camp is nearest to a square, but in many parts levell'd and defaced, so that I could not make a perfect Draught of it; however, there appears on the West side of it, three Rows of Ditches, and as many Ramparts of Stone and Earth, and on the Side towards the Loch, is a round Turret entirely analogous with Camp at Burnswork Hill. The total Circumference of it measures 2020 feet, or 444 paces [*sic*]. To the South of this camp, there is a large Morass or Moss....' Unfortunately, Gordon did not publish even his imperfect 'Draught'.

Maitland gives the length as 250 yards and the breadth 'about eighty', and says that it was 'fenced with a rampart and ditch on all sides but the southern which is bounded by Lochore, and a small rising of a semicircular form, representing a half moon', no doubt the 'round Turret' of Gordon. Maitland adds that 'within the camp is the remains of an ancient chapel'. On the Ordnance map it is called 'Chapel of Inchgall'.

Bishop Pococke visited the site in 1760. The writer of the *O.S.A.* adds nothing to Gordon's description of the 'camp' which he repeats almost verbally; but adds a record of the discovery of 'several antiquities, which are evidently Roman, particularly the head of a Roman spear', found digging ditches 'immediately under [south of?] the camp' to drain the lake. But we cannot assume from this that they were in fact Roman, and nothing is known of their present whereabouts. Are they by any chance still preserved at Lochore House?

Roy describes it as a Roman post 'of the stationary kind' big enough for 'a cohort or two' only. Chalmers adds nothing to Lochore, but records, on the authority of Sibbald, a 'great strength' with double ramparts and ditches, on Benarty Hill. Lt-Colonel Miller says the ramparts were levelled about 1817 when a farm-steading (no doubt the present farm-house) was put there. 'Upon viewing the ground where the camp stood from the hill above it last summer, when the corn was beginning to ripen, I could distinctly perceive the traces of three ditches at the north-east angle, running parallel to each other, from the corn being of a darker hue.' He adds that upon levelling the trenches, although the burnt ends of the pallisades were found, no bones, or arms, or any trace whatever of a battle were discovered'.

I visited Lochore in July 1925, and was able to locate three parallel ditches on the north side, visible both as depressions and as belts of darker green grass in a hayfield. The outermost ditch could be traced for a length of about 800 ft.; the western portion was visible as a belt of darker green oats. The other two ditches are visible only in the eastern field, for a length of about 400 ft. The outer ditch turns south-eastwards at the east end, forming a slightly rounded corner whose angle is rather greater than a right angle. At a distance from this corner of a little more than 100 ft. is a break and a causeway. The ditch then continues for about another 100 ft. where it appears to stop. The length of the east side is about 300 ft. These figures agree fairly well with Maitland's (750 by about 240 ft.).

About 400 ft. south-west of Chapel Farm is a clump of trees. On the west of this are three sides of an enclosure, visible as green lines in oats (length of sides about 200 ft.). There is a gap in the south-west corner.

The remains described and seen do not conform to those on any medieval site I know; and the fact that the chief medieval defensive site, the important castle of

Lochore, is half a mile distant to the east-south-east, on the other side of the now drained lake, seems against a medieval origin. But further evidence is needed before the remains can be considered Roman. The site, if still as it was when I visited it, is an ideal one for air-photography.

Sibbald, *Roman Antiquities*, p. 37.
Gordon, *Itin. Sept.* 1726, p. 36.
Maitland, *Hist.* (1757), I, p. 215.
Pococke, *Tour* (1760): *Scot. Hist. Soc.* I (1887), p. 280.
*O.S.A.* VII (1793), p. 315.
Roy (1793), pp. 82–3.
Chalmers, I (1807), pp. 110, 168.
*Arch. Scotica*, (1857), IV, p. 26 (paper by Lt-Col. Miller, read 1829–30).
Knox, *Tay Basin* (1831), p. 4.
*N.S.A.* IX (1837), p. 446.
Watson, *Celtic Place-names*, p. 247.
*Royal Commission Report, Fife* (1933), no. 57.

**Auchterderran** (27 s.w.?). The exact site is unknown. I have looked for it in vain on the ground; but it is of the kind that might well be rediscovered in a few minutes by air-reconnaissance. It is thus described in 'a manuscript account of General Melville's search for Roman camps in Scotland, compiled about 1812 by his secretary John Dougall, and now in the possession of Mr E. W. M. Balfour-Melville'. The account says: 'About a couple of miles to the eastward of that station [Lochore], on a gentle eminence, vestiges of a rampart and ditch, forming the south-west angle of a rectangular and rectilinear inclosure, have been noticed; and within the inclosure was found, about fifty years ago, a silver coin of Pertinax.' If this was a Roman camp or fort it must, on the evidence of the coin, belong to a period after A.D. 193, or at any rate have been occupied after that date. This is the only record of the discovery of a coin of Pertinax in Scotland. It would seem to have been somewhere near Pitkinny.

*P.S.A.S.* LII (1918), p. 238; Sir George Macdonald quoting his own article in *Archaeologia* LXVIII (1917), pp. 169 ff. See also p. 58 above.

**Nuthill, Falkland** (19 N.W.). The *O.S.A.* says: 'On the east of Nuthill, and nearly half a mile west of the house [of Falkland], are four parallel trenches, in the form of inverted wedges, of from 250 to 300 yards in length.' This suggests traffic-ruts of an old road, and they are probably those marked on the map at Chancefield.

*O.S.A.* IV (1792), p. 449.

**Carnock** (38 N.E.). The *O.S.A.* speaks of 'a camp a little south from the village of Carnock, upon an eminence, which still retains the name of Camps'. I visited the site in 1925, and came to the conclusion that it was more likely to be medieval than Roman, but it is much defaced.

*O.S.A.* XI (1794), p. 497.
*Arch. Scot.* IV (1857), p. 25.

## INVERNESS-SHIRE

**Dochen** (19 N.E.). This site lies on a projecting tongue of low-lying land between Loch Ness and Loch Dochfour. Here two sites are marked on the Ordnance map and described as the 'site of the Roman station called Banatia', which, as we have seen (p. 44), is more probably to be identified with Dalginross. They were described in some detail in 1822, and are evidently not Roman (though I have not seen them); they consist of two small square forts, one of which 'has the appearance of being built with modern masonry. It is twenty-four paces on each side.'

> Chalmers, I (1807), p. 179, note C, quoting—
> *Survey of Moray*, p. 53.
> *Arch. Scotica*, II (1822), p. 35.

**Kingussie.** The *O.S.A.* speaks of 'the appearance of a Roman encampment...on a moor, between the bridge of Spey and Pitmain'. Near it was found an urn full of burnt ashes, and somewhere in the neighbourhood 'a Roman tripod'. This latter was no doubt a medieval 'camp-kettle'.

> *O.S.A.* III (1792), p. 43.

## KINCARDINESHIRE

**Montrose's Trench, Banchory-Ternan** (5 S.W.). The *N.S.A.* refers to an encampment 'not far from the entrance of the Howe of Corrichie, called "Montrose's dike"'. It is on the north side of the road from Torphins to Aberdeen, between the fifteenth and sixteenth milestones from Aberdeen, opposite a mill-dam that is fed by an artificial mill-lade from the Corrichie Burn. The same lade passes close by the western side of the 'trench' and would appear to have kept it wet. The remains (which I have not seen) are marked on the map as three sides of a square-ditched enclosure, the fourth side having apparently been obliterated by the aforesaid road. The internal diameter of the enclosed platform, measured on the map, is about 200 ft. It would appear to be a medieval moated house-site.

> *N.S.A.* XI (1845), p. 341.

**Cairnton, Banchory-Ternan** (8 N.E.). The *N.S.A.* describes this earthwork in some detail. It was of 'massive structure' and consisted of 'two ramparts of earth, each 100 yards long, from ten to fifteen yards high [*sic*], and sixteen broad. They converge from the bank [of the Dee] on each side, and complete two sides of a square, the rest of which is formed by the nature of the ground. They do not, however, meet, but leave an entrance at the angle about twenty yards wide.' The length of the north-west rampart, as measured on the 6 in. map, is about 400 ft., and of the north-east about 280 ft. The site is in a wood, part of the great old wood of Trustach, on a promontory between the Dee on the south and the burn of Canny on the north. The ramparts, as marked on the map, are not perfectly straight, and the gap in the north corner, if original, conclusively rules out a Roman origin. The site is similar to that of Cardean (p. 88) and is worth investigation, though I doubt whether it will prove to be Roman; I have not seen it.

A hill $1\frac{1}{4}$ miles to the east-north-east, east of East Mains and the railway, bears the suggestive name Silver Craig.

N.S.A. XI (1845), p. 335.

## ROSS AND CROMARTY

**Port a' Chaisteil** (30 N.W., N.E.). The Rev. Mr Grant, minister of Boharn, described 'a beautiful square fortification of about an hundred paces of a side' near this place, probably that indicated on the map as the site of a Roman camp. It seems to have been cultivated since the minister wrote, but there may be some traces of it still visible. I have not visited the site, which is on the peninsula ending in Tarbat Ness and not far from it.

Arch. Scotica, II (1822), pp. 39, 40.

## PERTHSHIRE

**Flanders Moss** (131 N.W.). There are two large peat-bogs both called by this name. One is 4 miles south-east of Aberfoyle and is crossed by the branch railway-line connecting that place with the Forth and Clyde Junction Railway at Buchlyvie. The other lies between 2 and 3 miles east by north of the former, between the Goodie and the Forth. The earthwork, called 'camp' on the Ordnance map, is on its western side at a place where a tongue of hard ground projects eastwards into the bog. It was planned and described by Dr Christison who correctly regarded it as of medieval or later date. It consists of a four-sided plateau whose sides are, according to Dr Christison, 65, 67, 72 and 83 ft. long, separated by a wide moat from the outer rampart. There are remains of a bank round the plateau on the south and east sides. Though often described as a Roman fort, it is quite certainly of much later date.

P.S.A.S. XL (1906), pp. 20-2 (plan).

## STIRLINGSHIRE

**Abbey Crag** (N. 11 S.E.). The Ordnance map marks a square enclosure on this hill and some accounts speak of a 'square fortification' here. Miss Maclagan's description, however, makes it plain that there was a native (vitrified?) fort. What appears to have been a small hoard of eleven bronze spears (axes?) was found on the hill in 1784. I have not visited the site and from the air it cannot be seen on account of trees. The hideous Wallace monument has no doubt caused the destruction of much of the prehistoric fort.

Macfarlane, *Geogr. Collections*, I (1724), p. 136.
Pococke, *Tour* (1760): *Scot. Hist. Soc.* I (1887), p. 290.
William Nimmo, *Hist. of Stirlingshire*, 3rd ed. (1880), I, pp. 372-3.
P.S.A.S. IX (1872), p. 39 (Miss Maclagan).

**The Hills of Dunipace** (N. 24 s.w.). The name of Dunipace suggested to Buchanan an explanation of the origin of two entirely natural glacial mounds there. They were the Hills of Peace (*duni pacis*), or, as he phrased it, 'Emblems of Reconciliation'! They were 'placed, as it were, at the Fag-end of the World', and commemorate the termination of the Roman Empire, and the peace which ensued. Gordon, on the other hand, regarded them as 'exploratory Castles' of Agricola; and after twice describing them as 'artificial Mounts', then says that one 'is supposed to be natural'. Maitland, whose good sense was unusual and has been inadequately appreciated, effectively disposes of Buchanan's 'wild account', adding that there was a ditch round the top of the eastern of the two; but as both had then recently been planted with fir-trees, the ditch may have been made, as often, to protect the trees. I have seen the hills; they are both of natural origin, being the isolated remnants of a fluvio-glacial terrace, the rest of which has been eroded away by water action. Neither mound now has any defensive or other works upon it. They are connected by a low natural ridge.

The name, which Maitland spells 'Dunipass', may be connected with the word 'bass' which occurs in the Bass Rock and the Bass of Inverurie, both conical hills, the one of course natural and far larger, but similar in shape, the other a castle-mound.

The old road up the Carron valley passed close to the hills, on the north side. Between them is the old site of the church.

Nimmo's nineteenth-century editor provides an excellent example of the formation of a spurious tradition. Buchanan's ridiculous theory is quoted (without reference to him or his book) as 'the common account given of these...mounds'. Thus does a bookish invention usurp the place of genuine folk-lore. The next stage is reached when this story is given as traditional and cited as having historical value. There are usually four phases in the formation of such spurious accounts:

(1) A genuine, if usually impossible, account is given locally of observed facts that demand explanation: e.g. burials found, being not in consecrated ground, must be the result of a battle.
(2) This authentic but vague account is seized by someone with a knowledge of the bare facts of history and used to embellish it.
(3) The resulting mixture is accepted locally as genuine history, and the site of the battle recorded, often with a date, on the Ordnance map.
(4) The story is told as evidence of the persistence of 'tradition' over long periods of time.

George Buchanan, *Hist. of Scotland* (1582), 4th (English) edition, Edinburgh (1751), I, pp. 17, 18.
Gordon, *Itin. Sept.* 1726, pp. 23, 24.
Horsley, *Brit. Rom.* (1732), p. 175.
Maitland, *Hist. of Scotland*, I (1757), p. 207.
*Arch. Scotica*, I (1792), pp. 121–4.
W. Nimmo, *Hist. of Stirlingshire*, 3rd ed., I (1880), pp. 46–8.

**Arthur's Oven** (N. 24 S.W.). This was a round-domed building of squared stone and 'Roman construction'. It was destroyed in 1742 or 1743 (both dates are given) to provide material for the dam of the Carron Iron Works, by the proprietor, Sir Michael Bruce—'a sordid, insatiable and detestable creature' according to Maitland. The site is marked on the Ordnance map on the north slopes of the Carron valley a quarter of a mile north-west of Carron bridge. Between them is the Carron Iron Works, and to the west and south-west the artificial lake from which power is obtained. There is now nothing whatever to mark the spot where Arthur's Oven stood except a fragment of wall built of mortared stones, obviously modern. Immediately to the north runs a deep traffic-rut pointing north-westwards, and aiming south-westwards directly at Carron bridge. There can be little doubt I think that this trench marks the course of the important medieval road from Falkirk to Stirling—the Great North Road of early times; for Larbert bridge is of no great antiquity. The fact that Arthur's Oven stood near this thoroughfare may account for its vogue in medieval and later times, which, as the bibliography shows, was considerable. In these works are several detailed descriptions, measurements, plans and illustrations of the Oven, which fortunately was well recorded before its destruction.

The name (now spelt O'on, in pseudo-Scottish dialect) is as old as the thirteenth century, as the Newbotle Charter shows (*furnum Arturi*). A variant 'hove' or 'hoff' suggests a distinct word 'hoove', a cap, night-cap, which would be a not inappropriate term for it. On the other hand it was also called 'the stone house', as the name Stenhouse itself proves.

The site is unsuitable for air-photography, but excavation might reveal some remains of the foundations.

## BIBLIOGRAPHY OF ARTHUR'S OVEN

'Nennius', *Hist. Brit.* cap. 19. The passage in question is a late addition and does not occur in the older MSS., Brit. Mus. Harl. 3859 and the Vatican Reg. Lat. 1964.

Newbotle Charter No. 239, A.D. 1293 (Chalmers, *Caledonia*, I, 245).

John Fordun (d. 1384?), Book II, ch. 16.

Walter Bower (d. 1449), *Scotichronicon*, 1447 ('a plebeis Arthuris Hove dicebatur').

Hector Boece (Boethius), 1465?–1536, Book III.

John Major, *Hist. Scot.* 1521, Book I (Julius Hoff).

George Buchanan, *Hist. of Scotland*, Book I (1582).

Sir Robert Sibbald, *Hist. Enquiries*, 1707, pp. 42–6 ('the vulgar call it Arthur's Oven').

Gibson's *Camden*, II (1722), pp. 1222–3 (woodcut, pp. 1223–4).

Alexander Gordon, *Itin. Sept.* 1726, pp. 24–32, Plates 3 (two views), 4 (plan).

Macfarlane, *Geogr. Collections*, I, 330.

John Horsley, *Brit. Rom.* (1732), pp. 174–5.

William Maitland, *Hist. of Scotland*, I (1757), pp. 208–14.

Thomas Pennant, *A Tour in Scotland*, II (1776), pp. 228–9.

*Archaeologia Scotica*, I (part 2), p. 79 (plan by the late James Gray exhibited at the Soc. of
    Antiq. 21 Jan. 1781).
Gough's *Camden*, IV (1806), pp. 96, 103.
Robert Stuart, *Caledonia Romana*, 2nd ed. (1852), pp. 183–7.
*Proc. Soc. Ant. Scot.* IX (1872), pp. 43, 58 (account of, by John Reddock McLuckie, 8vo.;
    presented to the Soc. of Antiq. 1870: reprinted from the *Falkirk Herald and Linlithgow
    Journal*).
William Nimmo, *Hist. of Stirlingshire*, I, 3rd ed. (1880), pp. 46–8.
*Archaeologia*, LXVIII (1917), p. 199, fig. 6 (original drawing of Roy's Plate XXXVI).
W. J. Watson, *Celtic Place-names of Scotland* (1927), p. 209.

# Appendix 5

## LAWS AND MOOTS

THE word 'law' is extremely common throughout Eastern Scotland, where it may be said to be the normal term for a hill. The objects so described are usually small round eminences of natural or artificial origin, but sometimes even mountains are so described (e.g. the Sidlaws). As I have already pointed out elsewhere (Map of Britain in the Dark Ages, North Sheet, *Ordnance Survey* [1938], p. 17), the word 'law' is simply the modern form of the Old English or Saxon word 'hlæw', hill, which is common in Saxon land-boundaries. In England it often occurs as a suffix attached to a personal name, e.g. Taplow (the hlæw of Tæppa), Cuckhamsly (the hlæw of Cwichelme); and in such cases it is reasonable to suppose that the hill in question was the burial-mound of the person named, such as was actually found at Taplow. Near Calne in Wiltshire the word survived, in the form 'low', down to quite recent times, as a term descriptive of certain flat-topped natural rises. But elsewhere, and everywhere in Scotland, its true meaning was forgotten long ago, and by a confusion with 'law' in its other sense, a wholly fictitious explanation was invented. From many examples available we may select one from Pennant's *Tour in Scotland* (II [1776], pp. 179–80). Describing the neighbourhood of Dunsinane in Perthshire he says: 'Here are also several Tumuli composed of earth and stones of a pyramidical form, called here *Lawes*. One of a considerable size, near a gentleman's seat, called *Law-Town*, is supposed to have been that from which Macbeth administered justice to his people.' The hill in question is situated in the grounds of Lawton House, in the parish of Cargill (Perthshire, 74 S.E.); it is about 15 ft. high, planted with trees, is called on the map 'Macbeth's Law', and may be either a medieval castle-mound or a prehistoric burial-mound, probably the latter. There is no reason to suppose that it, or any other such mound anywhere else, was constructed for the purpose of holding meetings on the top—an absurd idea. It was the name and that alone that gave rise to such an explanation, which in any case is inapplicable to a name like the Sidlaws. But, by a purely accidental coincidence, prominent hills were, certainly in England and perhaps also in Scotland, used as convenient meeting-places. The Hundred Courts, for instance, met at such mounds, e.g. the Hundred of Mutlow in Cambridgeshire met at (but not *on*) the prehistoric barrow called Mutlow.

A further complication is introduced by the double sense of the words 'moat' and 'mote'. Like all words denoting the results of digging—ditch and dyke is another instance—there is an inextricable confusion between the ditch or hole dug and the bank or mound made from it; so that the words 'moat', 'mote' (the spelling is of no consequence) may describe either the mound or the surrounding ditch. Confusion was worse confounded when the early pre-scientific etymologizers derived these words, not from the true French source (*mote*, a clod or hillock) but from the Saxon word *gemot* which is of Teutonic origin and is cognate with, and has the sense of, our word 'meet'. Thus the two false etymologies converged to produce a single erroneous explanation. But just as 'law-hills' have nothing to do with laws, so neither have 'mote-hills' anything to do with meetings, so far as the name is concerned. There is an intrinsic absurdity in the picture of a primitive community taking the trouble to make a large steep-sided mound simply for the purpose of meeting upon it and listening to the promulgation of laws by the tribal chieftain.

# Index

PLATE I

Section of Roman road at Glenochar, south of Elvanfoot, Upper Clyde valley.  (*See p. 4*)

PLATE II

Eighteenth-century road on Mendick Hill near Dolphinton, showing quarry-pit (with stones in it) on left. *(See p. 5)*

PLATE III

Eighteenth-century road on the moors between Black Fell and the Devil's Beef-tub, Annanhead. (*See p.* 5)

PLATE IV

Central
rib

Central
rib

Metalled surface of Roman road at Collielaw near Lanark,
exposed by Mr J. M. Davidson.  (*See p.* 5)

PLATE V

Strageath: the fort, looking west. (*See p.* 40)

PLATE VI

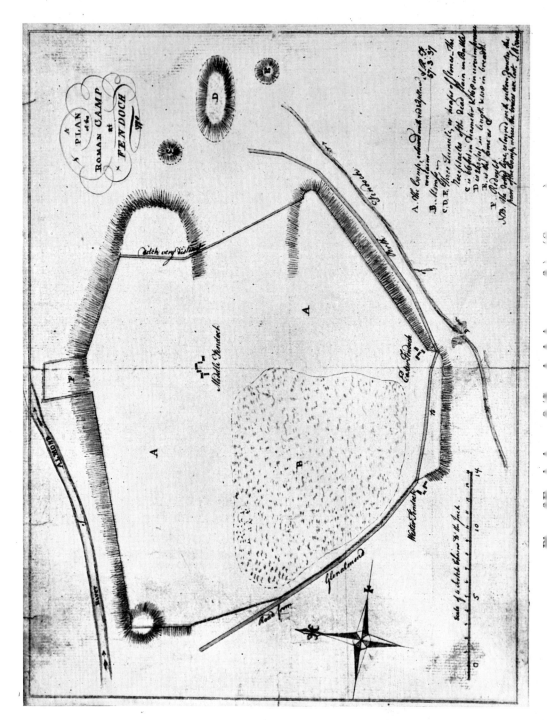

PLATE VII

Fendoch: the late Sir George Macdonald and Mr Ian Richmond at the
south gate.   (*See pp.* 46, 47)

PLATE VIII

'Bertha': showing the north rampart, between railway and river Tay.   (*See pp*. 59, 61)

PLATE IX

Grassy Wells: remains of rampart at north-east corner, shown by hump in track, looking north.    (*See pp.* 64, 66)

PLATE X

Grassy Wells: east side of the camp revealed by a crop-mark as a narrow dark band, with gap for entrance in middle. (*See p.* 66)

PLATE XI

Grassy Wells: south-east corner of camp, in top left-hand part, below large white mark; compare Plate XII.   (*See pp.* 64, 66)

PLATE XII

Grassy Wells: the soil-mark (white patch near middle) near the south-east corner; compare Plate XI. (*See p. 67*)

PLATE XIII

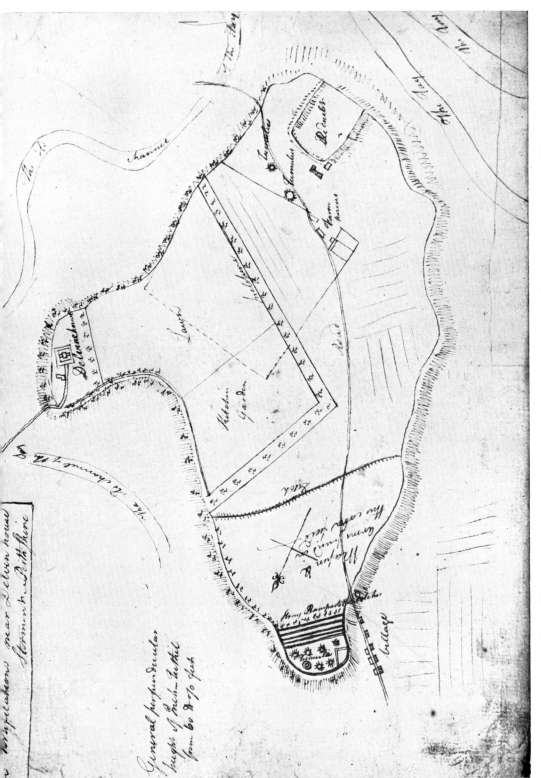

Plan of Inchtuthil, from the original, now in the Perth Library. (*See pp. 70 ff.*)

PLATE XIV

Steedstalls, looking south-west.  (*See pp.* 75, 76)

PLATE XV

The beech hedge, Meikleour. *(See p.* 79)

PLATE XVI

R. road

Parallel lines in arable (oats) between Westmuir (seen above) and Reedie,
marking course of Roman road. (*See p.* 90)

*(Photo: R.A.F. taken 1947. Crown Copyright Reserved)*

PLATE XVII

Kirkbuddo: the south-west rampart near the gate, looking south-east. *(See p.* 99)

PLATE XVIII

(*a*) Battle Dykes, Keithock, east side, showing depression representing the ditch of the camp (on right of fence).   (*See p.* 102)

(*b*) Near Kirkbuddo: outline of ditch of small fort revealed by a 'crop-mark' in grass as a white band.   (*See p.* 100)

PLATE XIX

Raedykes: the north rampart looking north-east from *F* on the plan, Fig. 27.
(*See pp.* 108, 109)

PLATE XX

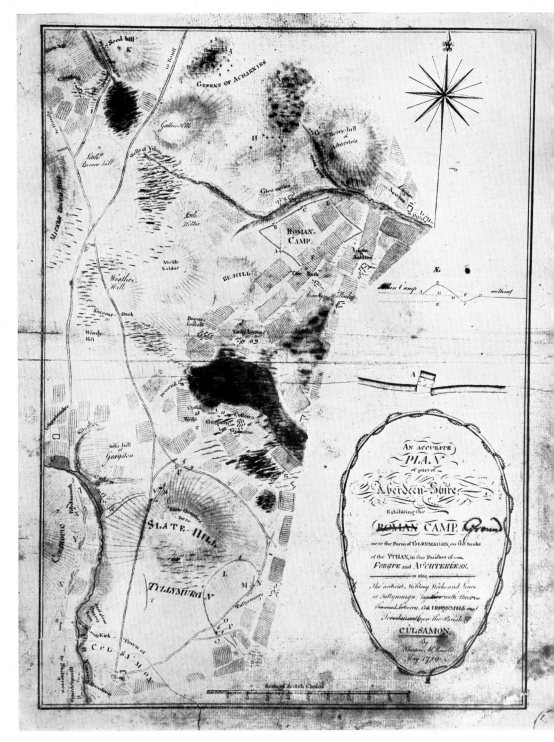

McRonald's plan of Glenmailen, 1789 (Scotch chain = 74·4 ft.).   (See p. 116)

PLATE XXI

(a) Glenmailen: the south-west corner of the camp, looking south-east along the south side. (*See p.* 119)

(b) Glenmailen: the north-east corner of the camp, looking north-west. (*See p.* 119)